Emotional Resilience

YOUR GUIDE THROUGH TURBULENT TIMES

BEVIS MOYNAN

magenta
Coaching Solutions

Copyright © 2024 by BEVIS MOYNAN

All rights reserved.

No part of this book may be reproduced in any form or by any electronic or mechanical means, including information storage and retrieval systems, without written permission from the author, except for the use of brief quotations in a book review.

Cover art by Jill Moynan.

Cover designed by Joseph Sale.

I'd like to dedicate this book to Jill, my mother whose creativity inspired me and whose artwork adorns the cover,

and Phil, my dad, whose consistency taught me so much without needing to say a word.

My mother passed away whilst writing the chapter on Sadness during lockdown in 2020. and my dad during the final stages of the book's journey with the chapter on love in 2024. It feels therefore only fitting to dedicate this book to them.

Contents

Foreword	ix
Book Mission & Vision	xi
Introduction	xiii
1. What is Emotional Resilience?	1
2. Understanding Emotion	9
3. Emotional Resilience and Awareness	18
4. Emotional Resilience and Stress	31
5. Moving Beyond Anger	39
6. Sadness, Loss, & Grief	52
7. Emotional Resilience and Disappointment	61
8. Fear and Anxiety	67
9. Unravelling Hurt - A Guide to Healing	83
10. Overcoming Guilt and Regret	91
11. Humiliation, Shame, & Embarrassment	101
12. Compulsion, Addiction & Emotion Cycles	105
13. Overcoming Emotional Attachments	117
14. Emotion and Physiological Pain	129
15. Restoring Mental, Emotional, and Physical Energy	138
16. Developing Emotional Resilience as an Attitude	144
17. Love	155
Final Statement	171
Work With Us	173
About the Author	175

Copyright © 2024 by BEVIS MOYNAN

All rights reserved.

No part of this book may be reproduced in any form or by any electronic or mechanical means, including information storage and retrieval systems, without written permission from the author, except for the use of brief quotations in a book review.

Cover art by Jill Moynan.

Cover designed by Joseph Sale.

I'd like to dedicate this book to Jill, my mother whose creativity inspired me and whose artwork adorns the cover,

and Phil, my dad, whose consistency taught me so much without needing to say a word.

My mother passed away whilst writing the chapter on Sadness during lockdown in 2020. and my dad during the final stages of the book's journey with the chapter on love in 2024. It feels therefore only fitting to dedicate this book to them.

Foreword

As a Professional Golfer with years of experience playing on the world stage, I have had the privilege of working on enhancing my Emotional Resilience with Bevis.

I first met Bevis in 2018 when I had just missed out on qualifying for the Challenge Tour grand final. We were introduced by my coach at the time. From the beginning, I was struck by Bevis's knowledge and desire to help me manage both my disappointment at the time and moving forwards my ability to navigate challenging and pressurised situations.

Emotional Resilience: your guide through turbulent times is a book which explores developing your own resilience through a growth of awareness. In a time when we are all bombarded by competing priorities, this book offers timely guidance on how to develop resilience, making it an essential read for anyone wishing to perform at their best professionally and personally.

As I read through this book, I found myself reflecting on my own journey and I believe this book has the potential to

FOREWORD

help you navigate life with greater ease and grace even during what appear to be really challenging times.

Bevis brings a rare combination of knowledge, wisdom, and experience of directly helping people to become more resilient, whilst also training other coaches in this field. This makes him uniquely equipped to tackle the subject of Emotional Resilience.

I wholeheartedly recommend *Emotional Resilience* to anyone interested in mastering how they react to pressure, stress, and the challenges life can throw up. This book will provide you with a series of tools to use to move forwards. I hope you will find that this is more than just a book: it is a journey into the development of a high performance mindset.

Yours Sincerely,

—Adrian Meronk, PGA Professional, LIV golf Cleeks team member, 4 x DP world tour winner, Polish Olympic Athlete

Book Mission & Vision

This book is both informative and practical, designed to equip you with a toolkit of knowledge to navigate your emotional experiences in life. The aim is that rather than being blinded by your emotions, you will instead be able to interpret them and move beyond them.

HOW THIS BOOK COULD WORK FOR YOU

Although reading the book is an essential part of the process, it's just as important to apply the learnings to your life. To support this, I recommend reading a chapter in full, reviewing the core takeaways, making a note of what resonates most for you, then completing the actions which accompany each section.

Occasionally, there are practical actions to take which will at most require your time and a pen and paper (or electronic device) to journal in.

I intend for this book to be an experience that inspires introspection, reflection, action, and integration—all key components of true transformation.

Introduction

What do you think about when you think of Emotional Resilience? Do you think of strong people who are able to endure incredible hardship? Maybe the willingness to help and support other people? Or maybe the ability to naturally allow emotions to flow in an organic and authentic way?

There are a growing number of books, talks, papers, and courses on Emotional Resilience, and it is understandably a topic of great interest in our post-pandemic world, where we are daily faced with greater changes and challenges. But before we try to acquire Emotional Resilience, we have to understand *what* it is and why it is so important. Then we can explore how to develop more of it.

In my experience, developing Emotional Resilience will support you in taking back the reins in your life, a journey which ensures you reclaim ownership of your emotions, mental dialogue, wellbeing, and zest for life!

In order to do this, we have to understand where the value of an experience truly lies. Does it lie in the external event or stimuli, or in our response? And when we talk about a

INTRODUCTION

"response", do we mean forcing ourselves to behave a certain way, or do we mean what we take away and apply to our future living? This book will deal with these important questions and give you the tools to apply these teachings to your life.

It is worth noting that although you may not have experienced challenges in all of the areas described in the chapter headings, we know that the stories, wisdom, practical activities, and tools offered will undoubtedly change the way you show up to your life. That includes potentially supporting those around you more effectively with some of the challenges that they maybe experiencing.

This book does not have to be read front to back. In fact, you could simply select a chapter title which feels most resonant and then venture into that area.

Whatever your approach, I hope this book inspires you to find your Emotional Resilience.

THE ORIGINS OF THIS BOOK

This book had its roots in lockdown 2019. Like many coaches, trainers, and therapists, I had been working both 1:1 with clients in person (sometimes online, makes me smile thinking back now) as well as in-person training (we also train therapists coaches and trainers). I don't need to tell you what happened next: the world turned upside down and we had to find a way forward. A third of all of our business disappeared and we had to find a new way to deliver the rest.

But what happened next was a surprise...

INTRODUCTION

After a couple of days of anxious thinking (no one is immune), I had a surge of energy and the creative spark to do something new, to get a new project off the ground, more than one in fact. The space that the lockdown created allowed my drive for innovation to surface. And so, we launched a series of Emotional Resilience Webinars with my good friend and colleague Callum Hardingham, helping people to navigate their way through what was indeed emotionally challenging times.

This book is largely based upon the content of those webinars, as well as years of experience using the tools of personal development, both pre-, during, and post- those lockdown years (because let's face it: the world hasn't settled down much since).

Now, more than ever, we all need to find our inner resources and rely less upon external input for our sense of wellbeing and contentment.

Everyone has bumps in the road: painful experiences, poor advice, trauma, major set backs, and honestly, this is absolutely normal. In fact, this *life history* is what makes you unique and as you may discover, challenges are required in order to grow stronger and more prepared for a thriving life in the long run. That is, of course, as long as you don't let these events define you and look for inspiration, healing, and support on your personal development journey.

This book aims to be part of that journey and to point you in the right direction, where you can continue to become all that you can be...

"Your story is either the weight on your shoulders or the wings on your back, you choose!"

CHAPTER ONE
What is Emotional Resilience?

What exactly is Emotional Resilience? Let's break it down...

EMOTION

Emotions are biological states associated with the nervous system. They are brought on by neurophysiological changes that are linked to thoughts, feelings, behavioural responses, and a degree of pleasure or displeasure.

RESILIENCE

This is defined as:

1. The capacity to recover quickly from difficulties; toughness.
2. The ability of a substance or object to spring back into shape; elasticity.

THEREFORE, simply put, Emotional Resilience is the ability to adapt to stressful situations and cope with life's ups and downs.

So, why is emotional resilience so important? Well, it's not just important: it's essential. If you strive to navigate your life without unnecessary stress, distraction, or mental and emotional obstacles that stem from a "victim mindset", you need to develop Emotional Resilience.

The second of the two definitions of "Resilience" offers us a helpful image to understand Emotional Resilience more deeply. Picture a sponge. No matter how tightly you crush a sponge in your fist, it always springs back into shape. *You* are that substance or object, able to spring back no matter how tightly you are crushed or how much pressure is placed upon you. We should note here that "back to shape" means returning to a mental and emotional state that is most optimal for the task at hand.

Life will always present obstacles and adversity. The goal is not to fantasise about a life without struggle, but to live in a way that prepares and equips you to face those struggles head-on with the words "game on" at the forefront of your mind.

Characteristics of emotionally resilient people typically include:

- Having realistic and attainable expectations and goals.
- Demonstrating good judgment and problem-solving skills.
- Being persistent and determined.
- Acting responsibly and thoughtfully rather than impulsively.

- Being effective communicators with strong interpersonal skills.
- Learning from past experiences to avoid repeating mistakes.
- Showing empathy towards others and caring about their feelings.
- Feeling in control of their own lives.
- Adopting an optimistic outlook rather than a pessimistic one.

Neurological research has revolutionised our understanding of how the brain creates and regulates emotions. In the past, it was believed that the limbic system, a set of brain structures located between the brainstem and the cortex, was solely responsible for producing and managing emotions. Recent studies suggest it's more complex than that. While emotional impulses do originate in the limbic system, our expression of those emotions is regulated by the prefrontal cortex—a cortical brain structure associated with judgment and decision-making.

This involvement of the prefrontal cortex in emotional responding separates humans from animals. Animals have little control over their emotional expression. When an animal's limbic system is activated, it will experience and act out the resulting emotion. For instance, a scared animal will instinctually run, hide, or become aggressive. On the other hand, human beings have the ability to make judgments and decisions regarding their emotional state and act upon those decisions, even if it contradicts their emotional state. For example, a frightened human can evaluate the justification of their fears and act in opposition to them, such as delivering a speech in public despite the fear of negative judgments. This ability to change the way we experience emotion is important for two reasons: first, it demonstrates our capacity to overcome uncomfortable emotions that don't serve us, and second, consciously choosing not to act on these emotions usually has a positive impact on our overall well-being and life.

Resilient individuals believe they can change their moods, their life, and become the witness of their thoughts and emotions.

KEY TAKEAWAYS

We have the gift of choice in how we respond. By consciously recognising this choice and actively practicing it, we can better navigate our life experiences.

Developing emotional resilience requires training. It is similar to training your body, involving exercises, awareness, and actions that, when combined, result in increased Emotional Resilience. It's not an all-or-nothing situation; rather, it's about enhancing your existing capacity for Emotional Resilience. At its worst, your Emotional Resilience skill may be weak and rarely helpful, while at its best, it can be strong, efficient, effective—a well-oiled machine.

One of the way to support the strengthening of that machine is the exploration of your beliefs: those that support enhancing Emotional Resilience and those that don't.

"Everyone always lets me down" or "I can't trust anyone", for example, are beliefs (however much evidence you have in your life for them, they are still just beliefs) which won't serve your Emotional Resilience. Beliefs act like self-fulfilling prophecies and as the old saying by Henry Ford

EMOTIONAL RESILIENCE

goes: "Whether you believe you can or you can't do something: you are absolutely right." Therefore, cultivating thoughts and beliefs which promote Emotional Resilience is a significant part of the journey to enhanced Emotional Resilience.

Some Beliefs which you may find helpful to adopt on your journey towards greater Emotional Resilience are as follows...

1. Life happens *for* us, not *to* us.
2. We are in charge of our minds and, therefore, our results.
3. We are only ever in control of our focus and actions, nothing else.
4. Our thoughts create our experiences.
5. We always have a choice.
6. We can decide how our story defines us.
7. We can become the conscious authors of our lives.

Pause for a moment and reflect on the beliefs above. If you adopted wholeheartedly one or two of these beliefs, which would have the biggest impact on how you lived your life?

How would adopting that belief change how you approach people, circumstances, and situations in your life?

If you're not sure where to start, try exploring a belief above which challenges you the most in terms of how you naturally think about things.

Reflections:..

Limiting Beliefs:...

Once you have taken the time to reflect on the above, pause a moment further and reflect upon beliefs which you currently hold about the world which, if you were able to let go of them, or act as if they didn't exist, would help you on your journey to greater emotional resilience.

*Tip Any doubts you have about your ability, anything starting with "I can't", or even things which limit choice such as "I have to" or "I need to", can go into this space.

Reflections:..

TRAITS OF EMOTIONAL RESILIENCE

Let's examine some of the traits of Emotional Resilience that we can all access and work with.

EMOTIONAL AWARENESS:

People with emotional awareness understand their own feelings and those of others. They respond appropriately to others and regulate and cope with difficult emotions such as anger or fear effectively.

PERSEVERANCE:

Resilient individuals trust the process and don't give up. They continue working toward their goals even in the face of obstacles.

INTERNAL LOCUS OF CONTROL:

They believe they are in control of their own lives, allowing them to be proactive and solution-oriented in dealing with stressors.

OPTIMISM:

Resilient individuals see the positives in most situations and believe in their own strength. This shift in perspective empowers them to handle problems with more choices and an empowered mindset.

SUPPORT:

Social support plays a crucial role in fostering resilience. Resilient individuals surround themselves with supportive friends, family, and sometimes seek coaching or personal development training.

SENSE OF HUMOUR:

People with Emotional Resilience can find humour in life's difficulties, shifting their perspective from threats to challenges and reducing stress.

PERSPECTIVE:

Resilient individuals learn from their mistakes, see obstacles as challenges, and find meaning in life's challenges instead of seeing themselves as victims.

SPIRITUALITY:

Being connected to one's spiritual side is associated with stronger Emotional Resilience. This doesn't necessarily refer to religion but rather one's drive for greater meaning, contribution, and connection with the universe.

So, how can you train Emotional Resilience?

Specifically, by growing our awareness of our thought processes and our emotions and whether they help or hinder us. By understanding, identifying, and labelling our emotions, we can learn from them, manage them effectively, and adapt our thoughts and behaviours to minimise stress and maximise well-being and positive relationships.

ACTIONS & REFLECTIONS FROM CHAPTER 1

A good start would be to set the intention of noticing when uncomfortable emotions arise: What was the emotion? Where was it in the body? And what was the trigger that caused your internal response?

If you begin noticing and journalling these things, reflective practice will help you move forwards—and is a great accompaniment to reading this book. You may find in time you can identify the route cause of the discomfort and the pattern of behaviour which accompanies it.

Completing the two sets of reflections around beliefs in this chapter will start you off on your journey towards identifying how—by changing your day to day thought process—you can move towards a life with greater choice, openness, and transparency.

Finally, don't expect too much at this stage! Be kind to yourself. Simply by making the intention to notice how you feel in certain situations is a step forward on your journey to enhanced Emotional Resilience.

CHAPTER TWO
Understanding Emotion

Human emotions are diverse and multifaceted, displaying different complexities and intensities. However, they're not all created equal. Some emotions emerge on the surface, quick and ephemeral, like ripples on a pond. Others, however, are born of deeper, murkier waters, emerging as secondary emotions as responses to profound emotional scars endured earlier in life. These latter emotions are consequential, forming from raw experiences etched into our hearts and minds.

To illuminate this concept further, let's delve into an analogy that has often proven helpful with my coaching clients. I like to refer to this as the "River of Life".

Picture yourself in a rowboat, gently bobbing on a river that flows toward an endless sea. The boat is you, and the oars you hold are the tools you use to navigate your life. This river is representative of your life's journey, flowing with the current of time, and the sea in the distance signifies the vast, uncertain future.

Now, envision boulders scattered throughout this river, obstacles that disrupt the water's smooth flow. These boulders represent the emotional scar tissue you've acquired throughout your life. The more profound the emotional wound, the larger the boulder, the more disruption it causes in your peaceful journey. More often than not, the most substantial boulders, the ones that create the most turbulence, are born from profound experiences of sadness, hurt, or loss.

The wake created by these boulders, the secondary emotions, can be likened to fear and anger. These are the turbulent ripples and currents that upset your boat as you approach a scar-laden boulder in your path. When you take hold of those metaphorical oars, trying to navigate your way, you may find yourself reacting with defensiveness, anger, or frustration. This reaction occurs when the memory of a past wound surfaces, the echo of a hurt not yet healed.

Your unconscious mind, always acting as the stalwart protector, responds by generating these secondary emotions. You feel anxiety, fear, or apprehension when approaching a situation that echoes past hurt or loss. This protective mechanism, although well-intentioned, can often prevent you from fully engaging with various experiences that could potentially propel your life forward.

For example, consider how an individual who has experienced a heartbreaking end to a relationship may feel a surge of fear or anxiety when they start to develop feelings for someone new. Their unconscious mind, recognising the potential for a repeat of past hurt, triggers fear or apprehension to dissuade them from embracing a potentially rewarding experience.

In this chapter, we'll explore the nature of these emotional boulders and secondary currents in depth, aiming to equip you with the understanding and tools necessary to navigate this metaphorical river of life with more ease, strength, and clarity. After all, the boulders and waves of this river don't define you, but rather, how you steer your boat amidst them does.

In essence, it's our fear, anger, frustration, and anxieties that often act as brakes on our journey through life. They stall us, halt our progression, and prevent us from allowing life to unfold naturally. Ironically, these so-called protective emotions impede the natural flow of more profound emotions like sadness and hurt, which, if allowed to flow freely, could lead to the release and eventual healing of these deep-seated emotions.

Imagine, if you will, a world in which you don't need to grip the oars of frustration and anxiety so tightly. In this world, the waters of your river are calm, and navigating them is serene and peaceful. If we were able to heal the past, the turbulence created by anxiety and frustration would diminish, serving less purpose, and allowing for smoother sailing. Instead of fighting against the current, we could let our experiences, like the river, flow naturally.

Our River of Life metaphor illustrates the futile act of clutching onto past sadness and hurt. Such emotional burdens merely weigh down our boat, making it harder to progress downstream. By embracing these emotions, experiencing them fully in the present moment and enabling healing from the past, we can lighten our load. This process of acceptance and release is not only liberating but also allows for personal growth and transformation.

By doing so, we create space for new emotions and experiences. We open up ourselves to experiencing greater joy, love, peace, and foster a stronger emotional resilience for the future. We can appreciate the ebb and flow of life, its currents and quiet waters, its moments of rapid rush, and its times of tranquil stillness.

Imagine the freeing sensation of paddling down the river with less resistance, where the waters are clear, and your boat moves smoothly. The boulders become pebbles, causing little more than a minor ripple. The oars in your hands are no longer symbols of strife but become tools for steering your path toward peace, fulfilment, and resilience. This imagery embodies the liberation that can be achieved through acknowledging, accepting, and releasing our deepest hurts.

The river ahead becomes a promise of future potential, unburdened by past pains. Life's inevitable turbulence no longer tosses us around helplessly but becomes a part of our journey that we learn to navigate with wisdom and grace. It is in this healing and releasing where we find the keys to a more enriched, fulfilling, and emotionally resilient future. The path to such a future is not always easy but understanding that our emotions are a river—not a dam—can help us to release the brakes and allow life to flow more naturally.

In the following chapters, we will delve deeper into the intricacies of the major emotions that we experience in our lives. We'll examine their sources, understand their triggers, and explore strategies to navigate these emotional landscapes with grace and wisdom. However, before we venture on this deeper exploration, let's briefly touch upon the relationships between the emotions in our lives..

Among all emotions, one we frequently judge and struggle with is anger. Our society often paints anger in broad strokes of negativity, associating it with loss of control, hostility, and violence. However, we might be surprised to find that anger, despite its uncomfortable manifestation, can often serve as a useful emotional state, perhaps more so than other uncomfortable emotions. How can this seemingly destructive emotion be useful?

The answer lies in the inherent characteristics of anger. Unlike emotions such as sadness, shame, or apathy, which often sink us into a state of low mood or inaction, anger is typically accompanied by movement and action. It creates a surge of energy, a rush of adrenaline that urges us to react or respond. Anger often begets communication, albeit heated or intense, which can lead to the expression of deeply held feelings or frustrations.

This isn't to suggest that we should encourage or perpetuate uncontrolled anger. But recognising that anger can stimulate action and dialogue, we can learn to harness its energy more constructively.

Furthermore, we can measure our emotional state by assessing our level of thinking or the number of thoughts we're having. Our thoughts and emotions are interconnected, each influencing the other in an ongoing dance of mental and emotional interplay.

As we journey into understanding our emotions more profoundly, we can uncover their correlation with our thought patterns. We'll delve into how our thought processes can influence the intensity and frequency of our emotional experiences and, conversely, how our emotions can shape the way we think. It's a complex relationship, a co-dependency that frames our perspectives, our behaviour, and ultimately, our life experience.

As we navigate the terrain of our emotions, it's important to bear in mind that all emotions, be they comfortable or uncomfortable, serve a purpose. Even those we might wish away, such as fear, sadness, or anger, play a role in our human experience.

Take a moment to consider the relationship between your thoughts and emotions. If you indulge in angry thoughts, you start to feel anger; immerse yourself in loving thoughts, and love begins to bloom within you. This correlation may not be news to you but understanding that an 'Emotional Scale' exists—one that represents the quality of your thinking as it relates to the emotions you experience—is a useful framework for dealing with these emotions. Over 90% of my coaching clients have found immense value in this scale, and it has been a critical tool in many of my training sessions and workshops. For further reading on this explore Power versus Force by David Hawkins

Let's visualise this Emotional Scale: at the top, we find emotions such as peace and love, and as we descend, we encounter anger, apathy, and right at the bottom, shame. Each step on this scale represents the increasing complexity of thought patterns and the intensity of emotions experienced.

Level	Log	Emotion	Life View
Enlightenment	700 – 1000	Ineffable	Is
Peace	600	Bliss	Perfect
Joy	540	Serenity	Complete
Love	500	Reverence	Benign
Reason	400	Understanding	Meaningful
Acceptance	350	Forgiveness	Harmonious
Willingness	310	Optimism	Hopeful
Neutrality	250	Trust	Satisfactory
Courage	200	Affirmation	Feasible
Pride	175	Scorn	Demanding
Anger	150	Hate	Antagonistic
Desire	125	Craving	Disappointing
Fear	100	Anxiety	Frightening
Grief	75	Regret	Tragic
Apathy	50	Despair	Hopeless
Guilt	30	Blame	Evil
Shame	20	Humiliation	Miserable

Power vs Force: the hidden determinants of human behaviour; David R. Hawkins, M.D, Ph.D.

POWERFORCE

Why are feelings of deep sadness and depression positioned lower on the scale? The reason behind this is that these emotions often create a numbness, a detachment from the emotional experience. This numbness is a consequence of an overwhelming number of thoughts rushing through the mind simultaneously. It's akin to being lost in a thick fog of thoughts that is so dense it creates an apathetic, almost anti-emotional, feeling.

In contrast, anger, which is higher up on the scale, is associated with less complicated thinking and more action. Hence, it's considered a 'higher quality' emotion compared to apathy, shame, guilt, or depression. This designation isn't intended as a judgment on the worthiness of an emotion but merely serves as an indicator of the relative simplicity or complexity of the thought processes linked to that emotion.

So, why is this Emotional Scale useful? Understanding it provides us with a valuable tool for self-awareness and emotional intelligence. It assists us in recognising where we stand emotionally at any given moment, giving us insight into our thought patterns and helping us navigate our emotional landscape more effectively.

One core component of Emotional Resilience is being able to navigate up and down this Emotional Scale consciously and healthily, leading to better emotional health and overall well-being.

Before we move ahead, I would like to share a case study that involves one of my clients, James. This real-life account sheds light on the concepts we have been discussing and will provide a tangible example of how understanding and employing the Emotional Scale can positively impact our lives and relationships.

James was struggling with his relationship with his son,, who had been diagnosed with clinical depression. James frequently found himself frustrated and judgmental of his son's frequent bouts of anger. However, as he began to understand the nature of the Emotional Scale, he started to perceive his son's episodes of anger differently.

James began to realise that his son's anger represented a form of emotional movement—a step away from the heavy fog of deep sadness and depression. It was, in fact, a positive sign indicating that his son was striving to climb the Emotional Scale. This newfound understanding transformed James' perspective and improved his relationship with his son significantly.

On the other hand, James also discovered that judgment—either from self or others—often leads back to a cycle of guilt, shame, and subsequently, deep sadness and depression. This vicious cycle was experienced throughout his teenage years. Their story holds important messages for anyone living with, or supporting someone, dealing with depression.

ACTIONS & REFLECTIONS FROM CHAPTER 2

With this case study in mind, let's now engage with some reflective exercises. Take a moment to ponder upon the following:

1. Which is the secondary emotion in your life — fear, anger, or both?
2. What triggers these secondary emotions in your life? When do they tend to surface?
3. What are the deeper emotional scars that your fear or anger protects you from experiencing? Could it be sadness, hurt, or perhaps shame?
4. Spend some time journaling about past events that might be the underlying cause of both your deeper wounds and secondary emotional reactions.

These reflections will act as your springboard into the depths of the emotional landscape we will navigate in the following chapters.

CHAPTER THREE
Emotional Resilience and Awareness

When considering what emotional resilience is, we must focus on three fundamental points.

The first element of that foundation is understanding a concept that befuddles many.

That concept is consciousness itself, and the intention in this chapter is to explore consciousness in a way which is simple and easy to understand which then leaves you with greater clarity of who you are as a human being and how you can use that knowledge and insight to live a life of greater purpose, passion and peace.

We will also signpost other material you can explore to further develop your own ideas about consciousness. Undertaking your own journey will inevitably deepen your understanding. In time, you may be able to share what you've learned in a simple and easy way with others!

Helping others may be the furthest thought from your mind right now. When we are in a state of challenge, struggle, and trial, we rarely feel we have the requisite resources to help others and keep passing on positivity. However, though we may embark on the journey looking to improve and help ourselves, life has a funny way of turning that around. What we learn on these very personal journeys is usually of great value to others. So, please bear this in mind as we proceed.

CONSCIOUSNESS

Consciousness is a very complex topic that has been addressed by scientists, professors, philosophers, and spiritual gurus alike. It is as much part of the vocabulary of New Age mystics as it is quantum physicists. When I talk about consciousness, what I really mean is the lens through which you look at the world or more accurately the awareness of the lens we are looking through.

The vast majority of people believe, at least at the subconscious level, that how they think and feel is determined by external circumstances outside of their control.

One of the very first things that I learnt when exploring NLP (Neuro Linguistic Programming) was a model of the mind which helped me to understand that our feelings or emotions are determined not by outside circumstances and conditions, but instead by our own mind. Our brain is constantly filtering the information received via our five senses, and it is that very filtering process that causes an image to be projected onto our mind's eye that in most cases bears little resemblance to what we might consider 'objective' reality.

Consider the following examples, which may accord with your own life experience, for a moment.

When you've watched a football match or television program or perhaps a political broadcast with your partner, your friend, or your neighbour, you will experience it differently.

The Arsenal football fan will have a very different experience of the North London derby to the Tottenham fan. The lifelong Labour supporter will have a very different take on a political broadcast than a lifelong Conservative supporter.

In more recent times, we saw the radical polarity between the 'Leavers' and 'Remainers' in respect to Brexit.

We're not just talking about a difference of opinion, but rather, a whole different way of processing the same stimuli.

In any situation, a different fellow human could stand right next to you, arguably observing from the same angle, and yet have a very different interpretation of what transpired… This is why, in criminal cases, witness testimony is afforded acceptable parameters of variation, because no two people will ever see the same incident the same way.

A friend of mine once saw a fight in the middle of Nottingham city centre. He was on a stag-do with his friends and suddenly another man was attacked by a group of three thugs. The thugs fled no sooner than they had knocked the other man unconscious. Luckily, my friend and his mates were able to get to the unconscious man, put him in the recovery position, and call an ambulance. He turned out to be okay despite a nasty head-wound from cracking his head on the cobbles.

Every single one of the men on that stag-do testified that the attacker wore a white T-shirt, but my friend is still convinced it was grey to this day. Is he wrong, or did he see what none of the others could?

And this is how we are constantly processing reality. What I am effectively saying is that how are you are seeing the world is based upon your personal, unique mind-filters. These filters include:

- Values (the things which are important to us)
- Beliefs (What we believe to be true)
- Attitude (which is formed from our learnt Values and Beliefs)
- Memories with stored emotion (positive and negative) from past events…
- Our meta programmes (otherwise known as our 'personality')

These accumulate through your life and become the gatekeeper of your reality, determining what information you filter out. This heavily filtered version of reality is what most of us experience on a day-to-day basis.

What we know for sure, from neuroscience, is that the only person who experiences the world in the way in which you do is you! No one else has had your programming, no one else sees hears, feels, or makes sense of the world in the same way in which you do. Colour blindness is an obvious example of the way we cannot truly comprehend how someone else sees the world, and yet we know that this goes much deeper: we all represent (or re—present) the world in our mind's eye in an entirely unique way. We even see massive differences between siblings brought up in the same household as their filters develop from their unique experiences.

What all of this teaches us is that the mind operates more like a projector than a receiver and this has a huge impact on where we look to solve the problems and challenges we experience in life.

Most people, when faced by consistent discomfort in the form of negative emotions, aim to change external circumstances: they change their job, their partner, their house, the country in which they live, and yet unless they address the deeper pattern of thought and emotion and become aware of it they will simply take the problem with them. Why? Because if the issue is an ongoing emotional response to a certain trigger, the issue is actually present within the filters of our mind, and the solution therefore is found through firstly becoming aware of the pattern then letting go of it.

As one of my favourite mentor's once said, "You can't let go of something you are not aware of."

NLP AND EMOTIONAL RESILIENCE

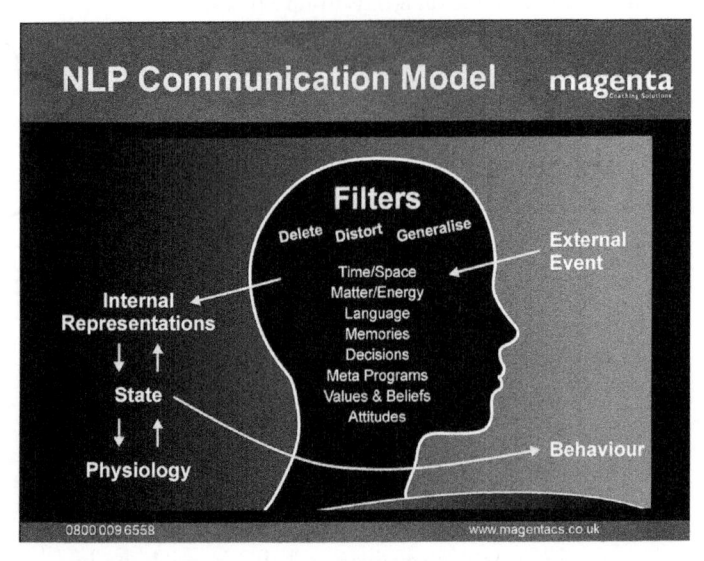

NLP teaches us that our mind deletes, distorts and generalises information coming to us in order to cope with the level of information bombarding our senses from millisecond to millisecond.

There are approximately two billion pieces of information bombarding your senses right now. Science tells us that what you can see, hear, taste, touch, and smell at any moment, what you can *actually* experience as a human being, is only 134 bits of information (or 3 to 7 chunks of information).

Having trained NLP for over a decade, it is always a surprise when we go through the exercises in the course to demonstrate to people that they themselves are deleting, distorting, and generalising information in a way which leads to them realising that they themselves are not experiencing reality. At least, not in the pure form previously assumed.

To demonstrate this, let's do a quick exercise. Please count the number of Fs in the paragraph below. Please do so quickly.

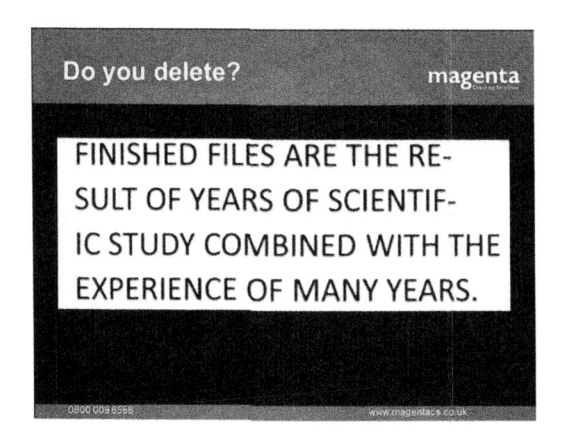

> Do you delete? magenta
>
> FINISHED FILES ARE THE RESULT OF YEARS OF SCIENTIFIC STUDY COMBINED WITH THE EXPERIENCE OF MANY YEARS.

How many did you get? 3? 4? 5? 6? Whatever your number, now take out a pencil or pen and just put a dot or a circle around the number of Fs. Now go through a little bit more deliberately. 90% of people, when doing this exercise, notice that they missed some of the data in the original exercise, and this is a good thing: we need to be deleting in order for our minds to work effectively.

Equally, our minds also distort information. Anybody who has ever experienced a phobia, which usually comes from a traumatic memory held either consciously or unconsciously, will relate to this. If you have a phobia of snakes, and you walk down the dockyards and there is a pile of rope on the pavement, there is a good chance that you will react, seeing that pile of rope as a snake.

In fact, how often have you been afraid of something that turned out further down the line to be absolutely nothing to be afraid of? In many cases, this can be a self-sabotage pattern whereby the unconscious mind is trying to protect you from previous emotional scar tissue and projecting the thought of potential danger into the present or future.

Finally, one of the other functions of the mind that is useful to understand is the mechanism of generalisation where, through our life's experiences, we generalise one piece of information to be like another.

This is an incredibly useful function, in that it facilitates many important skills, such as language. We can only make sense of a series of letters because of our brain's ability to create a general category of "letters", which in term form "words", which in turn form sentences and paragraphs. Without this skill, the little symbols on this page would not only be mere gobbledygook, but would take an eternity to decipher, because we would have to approach each one individually.

However, as you can probably imagine, our tendency to generalise also has drawbacks, especially when we take one piece of information and make it mean something which causes a negative emotional response. Remember, we are meant to be at peace and are thinking clearly when at peace.

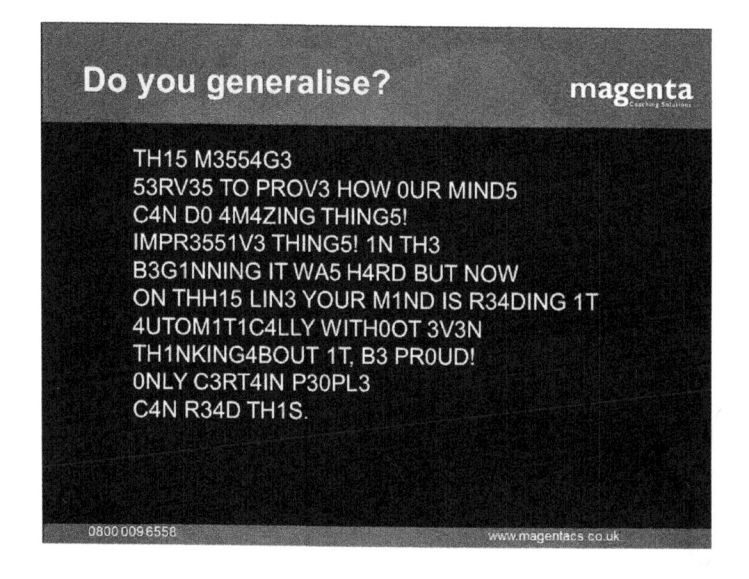

> **Do you generalise?** magenta
>
> TH15 M3554G3
> 53RV35 TO PROV3 HOW 0UR MIND5
> C4N D0 4M4ZING THING5!
> IMPR3551V3 THING5! 1N TH3
> B3G1NNING IT WA5 H4RD BUT NOW
> ON THH15 LIN3 YOUR M1ND IS R34DING 1T
> 4UTOM1T1C4LLY WITH0OT 3V3N
> TH1NKING4BOUT 1T, B3 PR0UD!
> 0NLY C3RT4IN P30PL3
> C4N R34D TH1S.
>
> 0800 009 6558   www.magentacs.co.uk

FIRST STEPS

So, now we have bought the concept of the mind as a projector rather than a receiver into our awareness. To recap: it takes millions of "Bits" of information from reality, filters those through values, beliefs, attitudes, and emotional history, and then projects them onto your mind's eye a heavily edited, somewhat distorted, and, of course, *generalised* version of reality. Worryingly, it is this heavily distorted view which most of us use as our primary method of making decisions!

Why are we innately programmed to delete, distort, and generalise information?

Well, apart from for the individual functions I've described, the bigger picture is that we cannot possibly comprehend or digest all the 2 billion bits of information bombarding our senses each and every second. We also have an inbuilt function that naturally wants to create associations between things; specifically, this function services to protect us. As a caveman, see a sabre-tooth tiger at the watering hole and then we link the watering hole with a feeling of anxiety and necessary alertness. This helps us to survive. However, in modern life now (for many people now), physical threat doesn't enter into our daily existence and as a result we find that the unconscious mind, when experiencing anxiety, is actually often trying to protect us from our own emotional reaction if something goes wrong. Equally, we will also experience anxiety at the side of a busy road where the unconscious mind is doing its job effectively in sensing danger to our survival.

You may have heard the term "seeking the path of least effort". Well, this is true in that the mind operates a little like a rockface when you pour water down it. The water will take the path of least resistance and in the same way our minds will fire the same sequence of neurons and patterns of thought and emotion associated with the same triggers. It's simply easier for the brain that way.

It therefore requires both awareness and conscious attention to create *new* neural paths and to make different choices. Only when they have been consistently repeated will they form a new more positive pattern, or "habit".

SCIENCE AND SPIRITUALITY

Quantum physicists long ago proved that the world is just energy and the chair that you are sat in can only be seen because it is vibrating at the same frequency as your body.

I recognise that with this statement we are at the danger of going down the rabbit hole, which we may explore later, but for now let's just accept that reality is far stranger than it first appears.

The really beautiful thing about developing greater awareness of this process is that we can use it to change reality. After all, we've established that how we view the world becomes our own protected version of reality. As such working on how you view the world really ought to take a higher priority in life as it literally affects everything!

At the very least, we can to stop ourselves from self-sabotage. By pausing to detach, to take a step back, we can realise when our emotions are giving us a clue that our filtering process isn't operating effectively.

In fact, it's now possible to understand emotions at such a deep level they can become your friend. We can now harness and use our emotions to further our aims and help others.

One question I get asked a lot during workshops, talks, and training is: if you're feeling good, are you thinking more clearly or less clearly?

This is a fascinating question, because in my experience nobody has ever said that they are thinking *less* clearly if they're feeling good. Everyone innately knows that when they're feeling good they're thinking more clearly. However, when we are in threat mode, we can often believe that more anxiety, more alertness, more tension means more awareness of danger. We fixate anxiously on things because we believe it will alter the outcome, when in fact, our fixation is likely blinding us to the full picture. The mind tricks itself into believing that feeling good is bad, because it means we are not fully alert, and are therefore exposed to danger. The lower brain is designed to keep us safe from danger, therefore the lower brain can never be the higher self, the true self, our *real* self. As a result, many people are suffering from avoiding threats which just don't exist. Deepak Chopra puts it succinctly when he says ninety-percent of problems are actually purely at the level of thought. In other words ninety-percent of problems are not actually problems they are instead just thoughts. Imagine what our life would be like if ninety-percent of our problems disappeared simply by growing our awareness! Sounds fanciful, yet this is the life which awaits you with time, reflection, and perseverance.

This is just one example of how what we *feel* can give us a clue to how effectively we're *thinking* and filtering information.

When we are feeling good about certain circumstances, situations, or outcomes, we can continue on with confidence. However, when we feel discomfort or fear, we can pause and interrogate the feeling a little more deeply.

How many of us have let fear stop us from doing something we really want to do? Or allowed anger to sabotage relationships? In both cases, being aware that the feelings are telling us we are not processing effectively can help us stop, feel the fear, and then take a breath and trust ourselves. This is how elite athletes cope with pressure, (as we saw in the foreword from Polish Olympian and 4 x DP World

EMOTIONAL RESILIENCE

Tour winner Adrian Meronk). Equally all parents can relate to feeling anger and then — from somewhere — finding sudden patience. Take that moment rather than acting on the raw emotion.

Emotional resilience, therefore, is partly about acting against our ingrained filters and learning to handle discomforting emotions

Our physical sensations and emotions give us a clue that our filtering process is either on or off track. One great benefit of being alive in modern times is that science, spirituality, and quantum physics are all coming together to form a new way of thinking. Ancient wisdom is being largely vindicated by modern technological advances, but with new and deeper insights uncovered by the scientific method. It is now possible to understand an emotional scale and how it links to our thinking.

We can all experience a huge increase in our quality of life by learning to understand the clues that our emotions give as to how and when we need to take a step back. Practicing detachment and making conscious choices will benefit us and everyone around us.

ACTIONS & REFLECTIONS FROM CHAPTER 3

Start making a note of successes and remember it is a mini-miracle each time you act against your unconscious programming and instead respond with greater awareness.

Secondarily, also make a note of when you react in a familiar way which you are not proud of and *also* celebrate — as this is now coming from a different place. You are on the change curve which always begins with awareness of the problem, and secondly includes the continuation of the problem behaviours before finally we take a new course of action.

Be kind to yourself as either of the above is a step forwards…

CHAPTER FOUR
Emotional Resilience and Stress

To talk about Emotional Resilience and not address stress would be counterproductive. That said, many people misunderstand and misuse the term stress when describing everyday life. For most people, stress is the experience of an emotion linked to a thought pattern. Although the emotion might be uncomfortable, with awareness, we should be able to handle this. However, the word "stress" is generally used to mean something far bigger and long-term that at times can seem like a problem without a solution, so let's get underneath it and deal with it now!

To start with, I would like to use the analogy of a plastic 30cm ruler, the kind you probably had at school. Now, you can bend that ruler by applying pressure. To begin with, this is absolutely fine: the ruler can cope with a certain amount of pressure, especially when you allow the ruler to relax every once in a while and return to its natural state.

However, if you keep the ruler under a certain pressure over a period of time, the ruler is now under stress, and you will start to see lines perhaps down the middle of the ruler which demonstrates the strain that the ruler is experiencing. If you apply too much pressure for too long, and the stress becomes too great, then the ruler will first become weaker and bend and then ultimately break.

I'm sure you can empathise with the ruler! I know I can.

But this pressure is not what we think it is. It isn't work or spouses or commitments. The pressure we apply to ourselves is actually *thought*. When we have repeated patterns of thought that keep us stuck in the same circumstances where we feel under pressure repeatedly, we feel prolonged negative emotions. And it is these prolonged feelings that create not only a psychological but also physiological impact, leading to a deterioration in health and wellbeing.

To demonstrate this think about the word dis-ease or literally to *not be* at ease!

I have seen back pain disappear inside 30 mins with a greater awareness of emotion.

Stress is the body's *reaction* to any change that requires an adjustment or response (i.e. the bending of the ruler). The body reacts to these changes with physical, mental, and emotional responses.

As cited in an article from Harvard Health Publishing:

> "A stressful situation — whether something environmental, such as a looming work deadline, or psychological, such as persistent worry about losing a job — can trigger a cascade of stress hormones that produce well-orchestrated physiological changes. A stressful incident can make the heart pound and breathing quicken. Muscles tense and beads of sweat appear.

This combination of reactions to stress is also known as the "fight-or-flight" response because it evolved as a survival mechanism, enabling people and other mammals to react quickly to life-threatening situations. The carefully orchestrated yet near-instantaneous sequence of hormonal changes and physiological responses helps someone to fight the threat off or flee to safety. Unfortunately, the body can also overreact to stressors that are not life-threatening, such as traffic jams, work pressure, and family difficulties."

Now let's examine the following definition of Emotional Resilience:

"**Emotional resilience** refers to one's ability to adapt to stressful situations or crises. More **resilient** people are able to "roll with the punches" and adapt to adversity without lasting difficulties; less **resilient** people have a harder time with stress and life changes, both major and minor."

So, how can we become better at "adapting to stressful situations" and not falling for the trap of "overreacting" to non life-threatening stressors? Let's look at the ways we commonly cope with stress.

STRESS PREVENTION

This is where we avoid stressors entirely. If we know that we get stressed out during a traffic jam, then we set off for work an hour earlier. If we know that a certain work colleague really annoys us, then we avoid them at the office. I want to make it clear that stress prevention is not a bad thing necessarily. Adapting your life to make it less stressful is really quite a sensible thing to do. As the Dalai Lama says: only a fool would continue to spend time with people whom don't make us feel good. So, taking this example, it is worth reflecting on areas of life where you can take decisive simple steps to avoid the stressor.

That said, sometimes we have no choice, like the many clients I have worked with who are forced to have a relationship with their ex-partner whom they still co-parent with. They can't simply avoid the stressor: they need to learn to become more emotionally resilient so that they can cope with the trigger and react from a different place. Their programming and past emotional scar tissue is suggesting one emotive response, but they must choose another. Sound familiar to you? What stress can you avoid through planning? And what do you need to learn to more effectively manage or move through?

STRESS MANAGEMENT

Learning to manage your stress, so that you can utilise stress to your advantage (as well as acknowledging how you may be habitually utilising stress to your disadvantage as well) is an important strategy for developing emotional resilience. A good example of stress utilised to advantage would be in public speaking and theatrical performance. Actors and speakers frequently talk about how they harness their nerves and anxiety in order to deliver a more compelling performance. After all, those jitters and shakes you get before going on stage or standing up in front of an audience are, ultimately, just energy, and if you can convert that energy into positive action, then you have more reserves than you had before! Elite sports people often reframe nerves and anxiety as excitement telling themselves that it shows that they care and the more times they experience this discomfort the more comfortable they become with it.

However, as with all methods of dealing with stress, there is a flip-side to stress management. If we over rely on stress and feel we need it for every activity, we risk overloading our systems. This leads to becoming an adrenaline junkie, forever trying to wire hype oneself up and override our feelings of discomfort, which, if done repeatedly causes inflammation in the body which in time can lead to dis-ease. We have to balance harnessing stress for positive action with acknowledging what our feelings might be trying to tell us. Have you ever felt like you couldn't switch off? If so this is a sign that you may have become subtly addicted to stress and may need external support to find greater balance in life. Many of my business coaching clients have ended up working to create a truly successful life, as opposed to one which looks good on the surface — and to others — but which isn't truly enjoyed.

STRESS DE-REGULATION

The final element is knowing practical tools and activities which support you in releasing unnecessary stress, bringing balance back to your system otherwise known as homeostasis.

Recently, there has been a trend of yoga tutorials on YouTube about "calming the nervous system". This is really the same thing. Our nervous system is activated by stress, preparing itself for a flight or fight response. But by soothing this hyper-active response, we can return to a calm neutrality that is less filtered and more clearheaded.

Everyone's way of regulating their stress will be different. However, it is worth mentioning here that even in de-regulation there are dangers of extremes. For example, alcohol is a common way many people—especially men—de-regulate their stress. In small quantities, this is not a problem. But if drinking becomes a habitual way of "de-stressing", then problems can start to emerge. I am not trying to be critical here, simply point out how in our attempts to deal with stress, we often compound the problem. As I said in the opening of this chapter, stress really boils down to an uncomfortable emotion, experienced very acutely. This, in itself, is not a problem, if we are able to tolerate the experience and investigate it for deeper meaning and insight and truth. The real problems usually emerge because of the methods we take to avoid, control, or remove the emotional experience.

Let's now look at some crucial belief-shifts which will support integration of the knowledge in this chapter into your daily life.

- Stress is not innately bad
- We can use stress to our advantage and actually often need a level to perform at our best
- Stress isn't permanent and can be changed quickly just as easily as our thoughts and actions
- We can learn to utilise feelings of stress as a clue to take time out to find greater clarity and be able to act positively rather than re-act with whatever is going on emotionally for us at that time
- Stress is often a signal of lack of acceptance and is a sign of internal resistance to what is, step back and soften your approach to what is, remember the past cannot be changed.

HIDDEN STRESS

To prevent or reduce stress we must learn to see its many masks and therefore not be taken by surprise when we finally realise it's occurred — often in most cases this realisation happens late in the stress cycle, when it can be a little trickier to alleviate.

So, keeping this simple, let's introduce the many masks of stress:

INTERNAL:

- Unrealistic expectations projecting stress into the future
- The belief that giving yourself a hard time will improve performance

EXTERNAL TRIGGERS FOR AN INTERNAL RESPONSE:

- Places which "add stress": too much time in busy traffic or in urban noisy environments
- People who, in this moment right now, create an internal stress response. In time through healing, we want you to be able to be around those people without the emotional response

ACTIONS & REFLECTIONS FROM CHAPTER 4

- Embrace discomfort and learn from the experience

- Utilise "Strategic Discomfort": aim to place yourself in uncomfortable experiences and journal the emotional response and the feelings that arise. Use the experiences to fuel your personal development journey with a coach or therapist
- Take actions to both learn more about your own discomfort and stress response and also to take a break regularly from stress
- Reward results of both overcoming stress responses and taking more time for yourself.
- Learn to meditate and make sure each day you have some time just for you alone
- What gets measured gets managed: when it comes to stress, rate the feelings of discomfort in certain situations. Grow in confidence as the discomfort reduces with experience. Sports professionals are excellent at this.
- Ensure your goals and visions include measured and monitored time for yourself, such as meditation or walking in nature (this is even better when made with a 12 week focus)

Choose one or two fundamental requirements to work on enhancing over the weeks ahead.

- Sleep
- Hydration
- Breathe (you are breathing anyway so you may as well learn to do it consciously)
- Nutrition
- Movement
- Rest and Fun (time to be silly, to laugh: laughter therapy is a thing!)

CHAPTER FIVE

Moving Beyond Anger

When considering Anger as an emotion, it can be useful to consider how anger affects us all in different ways. For some, it is experienced as frustration or irritation—and time is often the trigger. The perception of not wanting to be late is the cause of such stress—when getting the kids out of the door on a schoolday, or when rushing to a meeting while trying to juggle a call—that we "act out". These mild stressors are not necessarily a problem. However, deeper patterns of anger can be. I have worked with many clients over the years who had an old pattern at the start of the coaching journey which looked a bit like this...

Firstly, they present as someone who doesn't like conflict (who does, you might ask?). This discomfort, however, causes a pattern of struggling to be true to themselves; in many cases they appear to go along for the ride. This appearance of going with the flow is actually a lie waiting to bite. In the end, the frustration of not being authentically themselves leads to resistance, then resentment, and finally either an explosion of anger or outright rejection as they flee the relationship or the job in an attempt to escape from their own emotions.

The positive thing in this case is that simply reframing conflict to being true to yourself somehow magically makes the process of saying what needs to be said so much easier. We can then move away from the fear of how others may react towards us saying what we need to say for our own benefit and acknowledging how others react is one-hundred percent their responsibility. For many, these concepts are challenging but in time, with persistence, progress can be made. Remember each time you are true to yourself and break the pattern of pleasing others it is a mini miracle, be proud celebrate those personal development wins.

But anger can have deep roots that are not so easily pulled up. Let's take a look at a case study from my good friend Callum who was happy to share his story for others to benefit from. It is worth noting when reading this that Callum himself now is an incredible coach trainer and mentor to other coaches!

CALLUM'S CASE STUDY OF REPRESSED ANGER

Callum experienced anger from age eleven. I reference this because it is important to understand that our own deeper emotional patterns stem from childhood, and as we understand and accept that, we can begin the process of unravelling unhelpful patterns.

This is not to say Callum didn't experience anger prior to age eleven. However, this was the age when his relationship with anger took an interesting—potentially life-altering—turn.

Aged eleven, Callum's father passed away, and shortly after his grandad also passed.

In Callum's own words:

"My father and grandfather passing away truly blew up my understanding of the world and what followed was deep sadness coupled with confusion, frustration, anger and depression.

At that age I was not equipped (as you can imagine) with the awareness of how to express and process my feelings and so, although I did enter a grieving cycle, I seemingly became stuck for a long time.

Initially deep sadness was my go-to emotion compiled with confusion, frustration and well, anger. This then grew more commonly to the occurrence of depression and apathy.

It's worth noting that although my mother and both grandmothers were very supportive, they had also experienced deep loss at the same time and so it felt like a supportive environment in some ways as we would bond via our pain, yet, a difficult environment as neither one of the adults around me was free to fully show up from a detached emotional space for each other.

A long story short, the anger I experienced grew. It grew in obvious ways whilst also in somewhat insidious ways. Obvious ways were me regularly punching walls, slamming doors, shouting at my mother and others — all actions not to uncommon for many teenagers — particularly young emotionally immature males. My Mum at this point made a great investment buying me a punch bag which absolutely allowed me to energetically express whatever was required.

However, despite some of the anger I was expressing was perhaps a natural part of growing up, a lot was also fuelled by my perception of the world being a cruel, unfair, and confusing place. A place in which I felt out of control.

I didn't know how to come to peace with these events nor did I know how to navigate a life without consistent father figures and positive masculine guidance.

This job in part was left to my incredible mother whom absolutely was doing the best she could with the resources she had available, yet it was not her role to play.

I navigated the majority of my teenage years fluctuating from anger to depression. The in-between was numbed with alcohol and drugs.

Now it's important for me to say that it wasn't all bad. I have many happy memories of my teenage life and early twenties although all of these memories are also matched with lots of dark memories usually the result of repressed unprocessed anger.

Here's the point that needs to be made clear. I did not know how to consistently express anger in a way which felt like my environment at the time would accept it and so instead I started to learn to suppress this anger."

∽

IN THE WORDS of James Hollis, a Jungian Analyst and author, "Depression is anger turned inwards." This was certainly Callum's experience:

"The anger and emotions I taught myself to suppress soon resulted in depression. For me, this felt like a hopelessness, a sense that no matter what I do, the pain felt from the loss of my father will never go away and forever haunt me. Looking back, it would seem I lived my life in the fear of the pain's return, on edge, uptight and, from a purely biological standpoint, systemically stressed out.

This was exhausting for my mind and body and, as alluded to earlier in this case study, my vices of alcohol and drugs quickly became my only moments of relief from this fear, pain, and stress.

It wasn't until years later, after series of unpredictable emotional outbursts and occasional bouts of spontaneous depression that I decided enough was enough.

I came to a point in life whereby I would conclude that if this is truly what life is about, I do not want in!

As fate would have it, life nudged me in the direction of a few select individuals who directed me to reading material and information I had never been exposed to previously, namely the book *How To Think And Grow Rich*, alongside another book which discussed concepts I would later explore in my studies in NLP, such as 'you are in charge of your mind and therefore your results'.

These books really blew my mind. Not really in a sense of amazement but in a sense of pure hope and possibility that I may have a choice in the matter of how I navigate my emotional world and whether anger and depression would need to continue to be pillars of my existence moving forward.

I was a personal trainer at this time age twenty and although I was feeling inspired by the options these books were highlighting for my life, my entire focus was on becoming the best health coach I could possibly be. Not long into my journey, it became evident that in order to truly help people achieve the health goals I would need to solve the puzzle of the mind, as this would be what I would soon come to learn to be the source of all obstacles and all solutions. The mind of my clients and the behaviours, habits, values, beliefs, etc, held important were ultimately what was determining their potential for a successful health and fitness pursuit.

If they did not find assistance in changing the fundamental behaviours which got them in their predicament in the first place, they would find it immensely difficult, if not close to impossible, to change their health outcomes in the long term.

This being my motive, passion, (and maybe obsession), I searched for an NLP course I could attend as soon as possible.

This course would be the opening of a new chapter of my life and became the initial catalyst and experience which started to free me from my own emotional chaos.

Prior to this course I hadn't been able to speak about, remember, nor look at photos of my father without feeling sadness and anger which would trigger me and linger for days.

However, after a ten-year battle with these emotions, I came to an experience in a trauma healing methodology called Time Line Therapy.

This practice is something we now teach and it is safe to say it saved my life. You see, for the first time in ten-years I was able to talk about my father, look at photos, and share memories without being completely hijacked by painful emotional webs.

Why share this part of my story?

My inability to express anger and process anger was what led to the depression I experienced. Anger is actually a more functional state in comparison to depression, as anger at least has energetic movement and expression often implied. When I unconsciously chose to stop expressing or processing this anger, I unknowingly turned the anger I was experiencing inwards causing suppression and stagnation to occur which inevitably leads to depression (a cycle of deep sadness).

Time Line Therapy's core principle is that we must learn from events in order to let go of the emotions attached to them.

Expression is a huge part of processing any emotion.

Both expression and processing have to happen in a united way in order for people to move past a grieving process of any sort.

Now, when I look back on my own story, there were increments of time where I was able to express anger, but it wasn't coupled with an equal amount of influence to support processing the anger, the emotion, or the emotional cycle that the anger was contained within.

Considering the thought of an emotional cycle, there will be other emotions that precede the emotion you predominantly experience—in my case anger—and other emotions that come after it. You may just be more associated with one and, therefore, it may be more evident for you as as an experience.

Without getting lost in this area, what's important to recognise here is that even if you are expressing an emotion, until we process the emotional cycle and allow it to come to its full fruition, it will tend to repeat itself as a holding pattern. The holding pattern being a psychological function with the intention of not repeating the initial event which gave birth to it. In other words, we run protective emotional patterns to avoid experiencing the initial deep pain again.

This repetitive cycle experience was the case for me. I had times where I was able to express anger in ways that weren't of detriment to myself and others. For instance, my mum buying a boxing bag was by far the best investment she ever made. The boxing bag allowed me to just let out whatever was there, and it was therapeutic, absolutely therapeutic!

But although therapeutic, the core problem still remained and although I was expressing the anger, the underlying emotional cycle was still there and not being addressed.

On reflection, now I can see my father's passing was the trigger for a series of beliefs about the world. The examples below are not exhaustive but hopefully give you a flavour of where I was at the time...

- The world is not fair
- The world is not safe
- The world is a bad place
- The World is out to get me
- Life is short and I'm going to die young

As you can see, there were lots of unconscious conclusions that were made from the event and at the time I wasn't aware that I was living through these underlying belief scripts because I was so in them. Despite my lack of awareness at the time, they were undoubtedly prominent influences filtering the way I saw the world and processing the world's information internally.

As you can imagine, when I was living with the unconscious chatter such as 'The world is out to get me' at the forefront of my mind, I was living in a perpetual cycle of heightened stress. Heightened stress can only lead to one outcome when it comes to the mind: fragility and rigidity, and neither ingredient is helpful when creating a well-balanced wholesome life cake. As a result of this way of seeing the world, vast blind spots occurred, none of which were supportive of me being able to think outside of the box of my feelings. Instead, the emotional cycles were keeping me lost and, for me, I was lost in anger.

Over time, I found myself in environments where the expression of this anger wasn't deemed appropriate and, like most, I felt suppressed by this. Many will experience this unintentional or intentional scolding of our expression by those also prescribing inept social norms. I started to make conclusions such as 'anger is wrong' and, at the time, I unconsciously equated myself with my anger. I was essentially equating myself with being wrong.

The lack of expression of the anger I was experiencing led to the process of the emotional cycle being stifled. As you cease to express that which wants to come through you, it becomes suppressed, and suppression is an action that requires energy. Then the more you suppress things, the more you lead yourself into a state of depression. Suppression can perhaps be seen as the incremental action and depression is the result of perpetuated suppression over time.

What ensued was a state of hopelessness. A state of not knowing what to do, not feeling there was any choice. And this then led to some new unconscious decisions:

- There's no hope.
- There's no choice.
- Innately depressive conclusions.

Until I started to find new choices, some of which initially came in the form of mentors leading me to books, such as How To Think and Grow Rich, then other books in the personal development realms. Initially, I was directed to these reads not because of my own emotional healing requirements, but for the purpose of business and developing a mindset towards business and entrepreneurial spirit.

Little did I know, life had other plans for me, and these books led me to a new way of seeing the world, which couldn't help but imply new choices yet, at the same time, shining a light on new responsibilities that I didn't previously know were mine. Responsibilities such as: being in charge of my own mind and results in life!

You see, unknowingly, I was a victim of my own circumstances, via my own accord. And because I'd been playing a victim role and 'woe is me' thought themes, that was the way I saw my life. *This happened to me, and this is a disadvantage and I'm angry because of that disadvantage. I'm pissed because of that unjust event. Why me?*

This mentality can never fuel a state that really motivates you to want to take the God-damn reins in your life and do something about it. Let's be honest, if you feel that you have no choice in the matter of your life, why would you attempt to do something about it?"

∾

ONE OF THE presuppositions of NLP that is taught on day one really stood out for me and started a journey which continues to this day!

"You are in charge of your mind and therefore your results."

When you fully take this on board you stop blaming other people for how you feel and in time begin to see people who have and do trigger you as your teachers in life.

∾

READING this case study of Callum's, I hope that the need to avoid judgement of the emotion of anger shines through. It is the release and allowing of anger in a safe way which leads to an enhanced emotional state. If we avoid shame or guilt after angry episodes (both self-judgement and judgement of others), it is possible to move to a place of neutrality and acceptance much more quickly. After five-thousand plus hours experience of coaching and therapy, and training coaches and therapists, I am still yet to find a psychological problem which does not improve through the process of accepting the situation as it is. This doesn't mean you resigning yourself to it. Rather, accepting it as it is means you stop resisting life. From this place, you are psychologically in a much better place to look for and find solutions.

ACTIONS & REFLECTIONS FROM CHAPTER 5

- Be kind to yourself and others. Remember, anger has action with it; rather than feel guilty, apologise if needs be and forgive yourself as quickly as possible for any angry or frustrated reactions. In relationships, no one expects perfection, and the person who can recognise their flaws and mistakes quickly is the person most of us admire.
- Find a physical and safe way of expressing anger, go for a run, join a spin class, join a martial arts class, go to the driving range and hit golf balls anything other than repress the emotion.
- Learn to meditate and notice what happens to the anger when you slip into the gap (as it is described), transcendental meditation specifically can help you heal anger and frustration on a daily basis
- Explore the triggers of your anger. My client found hers the other day when she realised her pattern of defensive anger around feedback came from how her parents handled her and her brother making mistakes
- Book in to see a therapist or coach, ideally one trained in Time Line Therapy, to help you let go of stored anger and the other emotions which anger is trying to protect you from.
- •Sit still with the emotion and focus on your breath and allow the emotion to dissipate. If it won't by itself, then take that walk or go and meditate or journal the thoughts whirring in your mind. These activities will create a state change. Be mindful of

EMOTIONAL RESILIENCE

the egoic mind's propensity to story-tell in this situation and egg you on to feel like you are right and justified to feel angry. Remember, judgement is like drinking poison and expecting someone else to suffer. If you are angry, it is a sign that you are not thinking clearly, so keep that hand off the self sabotage button!

CHAPTER SIX

Sadness, Loss, & Grief

Whilst writing this chapter, I found out that my Mum was suffering from lung cancer. Rather than shy away from this, it feels pertinent and very real to share this experience and how I've tried to move through the cycles of emotion around sadness in a healthy and supportive way.

∼

MODERN LIFE ISN'T PARTICULARLY GEARED up for the grieving process, with constant distractions, demands upon our time, and an endless stream of work, family, technology, and expectations which seem to place constant pressure on us.

It is therefore very difficult in modern society to allow for a full natural grieving process to occur. As a result, I have seen hundreds if not thousands of clients and delegates on training courses who have not fully processed or worked their way through a full grieving process. This chapter is designed to help you to develop the knowledge, awareness, and understanding so that you can move through this process and, in your own time, let go of the emotions associated with past events to live the free life that those loved ones would want you to be living.

It goes without saying that, if someone truly loves us, they would want us to be feeling love and joy and peace and contentment as opposed to feeling loss, grief, and sadness. Despite this, through a complex mix of societal conditioning and expectation of how we should be feeling, many people experience a sense of guilt around letting go and allowing themselves to move on with their life many years after the experience of loss.

FORGIVENESS, ACCEPTANCE, AND SURRENDER AS OPPOSED TO RESIGNATION

True forgiveness is stopping the pretence that the past could have been any different. Acceptance is accepting things one-hundred percent as they are. Many people misunderstand acceptance as Resignation, the attitude that, "I can't do anything about it." This is quasi-victimhood, and not true acceptance. Acceptance is a case of embracing whatever situation is troubling you *as it is*. The simplicity of this is also its challenge. Acceptance reduces and minimises negative emotion around the issue—the extraneous narratives and commentaries that we add to events and emotions—which actually frees us up to think and see things more clearly, often with the result that we can take positive action.

During writing this, my mother decided not to take cancer medication that could have extended her life. This was, of course, one-hundred percent her decision to make. Perhaps a less mature version of myself might have resisted and tried to persuade her to take an alternative route. However by fully accepting and respecting and acknowledging her decision, I was able to move past any attachment to the outcome and instead have a discussion with her to make sure it what was she really wanted. From there, I could focus my attention on enjoying spending what time we had left together whilst also helping support in any way in which we could.

It's in moments like these that I am incredibly grateful for the personal development journey that I've been on over the last sixteen years. Whilst it is perfectly understandable for anyone to want to hold on to someone they love a bit longer, we cannot deny reality.

During the process of writing this book, and completing an emotional resilience webinar series alongside Callum, one of the things that surprised us was that we spent half the time talking about guilt rather than sadness. On reflection, this makes a lot of sense, especially when I consider the lack of time people experience for themselves in modern life.

It is strange how it is entirely acceptable to spend hours watching TV or with a phone in hand, however, taking quiet time to yourself on your own, to do nothing other than to reflect or meditate (or just be), is deemed unacceptable, a waste of time. It seems almost too difficult to either embrace our feelings. Or, if we are ready to face them, to have the discussions required with loved ones to ask for that time and make it happen. We all must acknowledge the tendencies of our minds to look for distraction from the deeper emotional pain that we may be experiencing under the surface. The problem with burying this pain is that it will inevitably come out later in life and often in a disproportionate response to the actual event that triggered it. There

EMOTIONAL RESILIENCE

are many examples of people being okay at the death of a parent or a loved one and then subsequently crumbling at the loss of a pet months or years later. These examples prove that the processing of emotion is inevitable, and we can consciously choose the speed with which we allow that process to occur. However, if we *don't* make a decision, and instead unconsciously bury the emotion, then it will be decided for us. I can absolutely assure you is that it will come back to bite you at some point in the future.

So, how do we develop healthy habits of being "self-full" (rather than selfish) and taking time for ourselves each and every day? If taking time for yourself sees too nebulous, let me give you a couple of practical examples of how you can let go of grief. This story may or may not work for you, but it is a starting point for self-exploration.

As I write this, my dad is eighty- six years old. His generation prided itself on the "stiff upper lip". Needless to say, it has been a real surprise to him how, in recent times, he has become more emotional. We put some of this down to the treatment he has undergone for prostate cancer, and some of it down to a growing level of awareness he has found later in life through using meditation as a way of relaxing.

When my dad lost his brother some years ago, he spoke at the funeral. My dad's personality is such that he wanted to plan and prepare the speech so that he would be able to deliver it not in a non-emotional way—which he could feel comfortable with. In practising that particular speech over thirty times he, in his own words, broke down in tears on each and every occasion. Although my dad's intention was practical—to prepare himself for the funeral—what he was actually doing during that process was allowing the grieving process to naturally occur. In this instance, therefore, we have a great example of how we can allow the grieving process to occur naturally. Let's break it down further:

• Firstly, there was a repetition and a commitment each and every day to practice that talk; so, there was a time of the day that was set where he was going to practice the talk and by doing so allowed some emotion out.

This is a commitment you too can make, allocating a certain portion of the day or a certain time of the day for reflection and quiet time for you to think of that lost loved one.

• Secondly my dad was also engaged in a creative pursuit: he was writing a speech. You can do the same. For example, you could try writing a letter to that person. I found writing poetry about my mum was an immediate release for me. Processing these feelings through words, whether it be a talk or a letter or a poem or any form of writing (even a text message), gets the thoughts out of your subconscious mind onto paper, which will allow you to experience, process, and let go of some emotion.

Of course, another way we can process emotion is by talking with friends, loved ones, or a counsellor or therapist about the loss and about the person whom we loved. This is an excellent way of releasing those pent-up emotions.

If we do not consciously release emotions, they will find a way to be released. Not long after that difficult conversation with my mother, I found my emotions coming in waves. I would have periods of days or even weeks where I felt absolutely like my usual self, and then the emotion would suddenly hit me like a wave.

In one instance, I was driving and I I hit and dinted my alloy on a curb. I pulled into my driveway and burst into tears. It wasn't the alloy causing the emotion (though I do know some people who feel that strongly about their cars). It was a signal: I hadn't been paying attention to my driving because my mind was elsewhere. The abrupt shock of the accident triggered a release to occur.

A couple of weeks on from dinting my alloy, I felt pretty okay. It's important to acknowledge that it's okay to feel okay through the grieving process: you don't have to be in emotional wreck all the time, so allow yourself to feel however you are feeling. This is probably the most important mantra throughout the process, coupled with giving yourself time for reflection and thought about the person who you have lost or are losing.

But despite seemingly feeling "okay", I was aware that something was beneath the surface. Though I was fighting it, I was feeling grumpy, dissatisfied with life (which has never been a normal feeling state for me), and "out of sorts". I went upstairs and committed to meditating for as long as I could in order to allow the emotion under the surface to release. After about twenty to twenty-five minutes (although I couldn't be sure exactly of the time) of sitting on my bed and going through a process of transcendental meditation with the use of a mantra, my mind quietened to the extent where I was feeling good, clearheaded. Then I became aware of a constriction around my neck, similar to the feeling of having a round-necked jumper pulled off your head. The feeling intensified and I knew I had to stay with it. I remained aware of this feeling and then suddenly came the release, like that popping sensation of a jumper coming off the top of your head. What followed was this beautiful vision of my mum in her early forties or late thirties smiling down at me, and of course, tears followed. It was a big emotional release for me and as I'm writing this I'm aware of a little bit of emotion left whilst revisiting this image.

I hope by sharing these experiences you can begin to see options for developing a self-full routine where you take time for yourself every day regardless of the grieving process. Then, if you are faced by grief, you have options. By doing this on a daily basis you can facilitate the natural process of grieving to occur. Do not allow fear to stop you: you won't become a blubbering wreck forever and will feel a lot lot better for allowing this process and experience to occur. If you feel like you are literally holding back a dam of emotion then it could be that you are also holding plenty of emotion from other experiences. In this case, I definitely recommend visiting a therapist—ideally one trained in Time Line Therapy™. I will provide access to materials and resources which can help with this at the end of the book.

Before we close this section on sadness, grief, and loss, I would just like to leave you with one final thought, and that is that you do not become sad about something which you don't love.

Sadness, therefore, is deeply interconnected with love in the same way that nervousness anxiety and excitement are deeply interconnected. Knowing this, at least in my view, makes the grieving process easier. Because what you are doing by grieving is going through a process of deeply acknowledging the love that you hold for the person who is no longer with us. By acknowledging things in this way, this process becomes an act of kindness and love towards yourself too, as well as a ritual of saying goodbye. Finally it is really important also to acknowledge that this process is equally as valid for losing a relationship as it is for the loss of a grandparent or loved one. If you have been in a long term relationship of any kind, when that ends there may well be a grieving process to go through. Equally, there may not be, and that's okay, it's just important to acknowledge that it is possible and therefore to allow a natural grief cycle to occur. This can be challenging and, as you are unlikely to get offered time off from work or other responsibilities if your partner leaves you or indeed if another life event sets you back, you have to find ways to carve out that time.

Examples of loss can take may forms and include...

- A physical injury or illness which gets in the way of you doing the activities which make up a strong sense of your identity, or indeed changes how you look which again is part of your identity.
- The loss of a job role or title which formed a strong part again of your identity and perhaps even your sense of self-esteem which was being derived from the role or position.
- A major change in career. Retirement from professional sport or leaving the armed forces are both examples where many struggle to make that transition psychologically from one lifestyle to another.
- Children leaving the family home can challenge parents who have identified heavily as a Mother or Father and now find that transition difficult.

None of these life challenges are likely to result in garnering support from the outside world, except perhaps in the form of a sympathetic friend or colleague, yet the grief process is still present. It is therefore really important to be kind to yourself and allow yourself both the time to grieve and give yourself the same guidance and support you would your best friend!

Be kind, gentle, supportive and please do seek help if you feel you are being affected by any of the issues raised in this chapter. There is guidance at the back of the book where we can signpost you for further support if you feel you would benefit from that.

So, take this time now be kind to yourself and be self-full.

ACTIONS & REFLECTIONS FROM CHAPTER 6

- **Book in time to actively grieve** using the tips from this chapter: set a time and commit to a daily practice and learn what works for you to help release sadness.
- **Talk to others about your experience.** You are not alone in your experience and a problem shared is a problem halved…
- **Book in to see a counsellor, therapist, and / or coach** to talk through your experience and actively release the emotion.
- **Be okay with being okay.** Many people on a personal development or spiritual path may find themselves not in the need of as much time grieving as they see this as the natural cycle of life and death of the physical body not the true self. It's important that you are ok with being okay even if society tells you you should be feeling a certain way.

CHAPTER SEVEN
Emotional Resilience and Disappointment

Sadness and disappointment may not, at first glance, seem to be closely linked. But for those of us who work in personal development and therapy, they are very similar. Sadness is often an internalised feeling linked to the loss of something or someone outside of the self, whereas disappointment is an internal feeling of discomfort linked to a perception of not living up to our own expectations. In this way, they are both expressions of loss, though sadness is focused on something lost outside of us such as a loved one or relationship. Disappointment is a reaction to an event not going as we had intended. My work with professional golfers has often centred around handling disappointment and becoming more resilient to the ups and downs of an incredibly difficult sport.

In this way, disappointment is often trickier to deal with than sadness. Sadness and loss and grief will naturally dissipate if we allow time for the grieving process. However, disappointment in ourselves is an ongoing learnt pattern which can be tricky to move beyond. The pattern of learning to be hard on yourself and to set unreasonable expectations is something that I have seen plague clients, family members, elite sports people, close friends and to be honest myself!

So, let's explore where this pattern comes from…

At some point during our formative years, achievement starts becoming a thing, whether that be in sport, academia, or the arts. At this point, we learn to raise the bar of expectation level which, from a performance perspective, is a good idea.

Jack Nicholas famously said that golf was a game of ever-increasing expectation which, for those who want to improve as golfers, is inevitably true. So, why is it then that I know of many golf professionals who have given up the game because of the frustration and disappointment they experience in shooting a round of golf in their seventies which ninety-nine percent of golfers would be very happy with?

The problem here is that the expectation levels have lost track with reality, and in this context professional golfers who now no longer play the game regularly but instead coach for a living find it hard to perform and enjoy the game at a lower level.

In a different context, I had a conversation with a good friend of mine recently whose son had achieved fantastic exam results, yet ended up in tears with the one grade which was below top mark. My daughter, who is a fantastic dancer, ran off stage recently at a competition at the end of her routine and burst into tears as she hadn't performed the routine as she had set out in her mind. She was really upset and disappointed and her mum and her teacher did a great job of calming her down and reassuring her so that she could enjoy the rest of the day and her remaining dances. What happened next was a beautiful life-teaching moment in that when it came to the scoring for her dance—that she felt she hadn't performed well—she was placed first! In her mind, she was super disappointed yet the reality was that she had performed and danced beautifully. Sometimes we can trick ourselves into thinking that only perfection will suffice where as in reality perfection is unattainable and we literally can only do our best moment to moment.

"Everyone is doing the best they can with what they have."

We have been hoodwinked into believing that seeking perfection, and perfectionist tendencies, is what leads to top performance. But this is only partially true. There is also an inherent danger here which needs to be avoided. Jack Nicholas's quote needs greater context for full understanding of what leads to elite performance (beyond the obvious aptitude and application).

Golf and life are indeed experiences of ever increasing expectation which when coupled with *detachment from the outcome* can lead to longer term success.

This is how top performers keep performing in business and life and sport at a high level; they learn to trust the process and let go of the outcome so that they do not experience overwhelming disappointment at finishing second, fifth or even last.

Why else do we see amazing moments of sportsmanship from those who ostensibly have been defeated? It's because top performers relish the process of the battle itself rather than the end result, just as top business people relish the process of taking the product to market and learn to detach from the outcome and trust that the outcome will be the right thing. They focus instead upon what will be learnt as opposed to success or failure.

One of my favourite—and perhaps the most transformational of the neuro-linguistic programming presuppositions—is that:

"There is no such thing as failure only feedback."

If you believe, as many top performers do, that failure doesn't exist, and instead focus on what there is to learn, then life becomes an infinite journey of self improvement.

This is the mindset of the top performer and it has to be in order for them to cope with the inevitable ups and downs of putting oneself out there in the firing line of judgement, criticism, and perceived success or failure. When you enter into life with this attitude, life becomes a win-win. Either you perform well and live up to expectations or you don't and you learn something from it which helps you to improve performance in the future. By adopting this attitude we avoid holding onto more and more emotion around disappointment. Many people experience this emotion building up as one perceived disappointment leads to another. In many cases, this is a learnt pattern from childhood and often picked up from parents. However, the good news is it can be un-learnt just as easily with greater awareness and a commitment to the personal development journey.

If we adopt the perfectionist approach, and are hard on ourselves and beat ourselves up for our perceived failings and inadequacies, then what we can find ourselves in is a cycle involving disappointment, expectation, and anxiety. When you have a pattern of being hard on yourself then your unconscious mind may well try and protect you from that emotion by creating anxiety in advance. This places you on high alert that a potential threat is on the horizon. In this instance, the threat isn't a real physical threat, but is actually the threat of our own emotions of disappointment.

So, learning to be mindful around disappointment and learning to learn from perceived failure is hugely important, not only for emotional health but also to experience lower levels of anxiety.

USEFUL BELIEFS TO HELP OVERCOME AND DEAL WITH DISAPPOINTMENT AND ANXIETY.

- There is no such thing as failure only feedback
- Judging others is like drinking poison and expecting someone else to suffer
- Taking time to grieve, reflect, or meditate is self-full not selfish
- Forgiveness is the process of no longer pretending the past could have been any different…
- Acceptance is fully accepting situations and events as they are (no longer resisting what is)

ACTIONS & REFLECTIONS FROM CHAPTER 7

- **Catch your high expectations and check is that realistic?** is it actually helping you to perform and live life in a balanced way?
- **Set positive intentions which replace previously high expectations** which you had to meet:

intentions are softer, gentler. It is an intention without a must, have, or should involved…
- **Change timescale with greater realism** and allow more time for yourself both during the day, week, month and year. Remember, success is a feeling not an outcome!

CHAPTER EIGHT
Fear and Anxiety

Fear is one of the most fundamental of emotions, designed long ago to protect us from threats to our survival. In today's world, these life-or-death situations are far less common, yet many of us struggle with fears that hold us back from fully engaging in life. Think about it for a moment have you ever let fear stop you from doing something which you really wanted to do?

In this chapter, we will take a comprehensive look at the root causes of fear, its effect on the mind and body, and most importantly, provide proven techniques to help understand and master fear. By facing our fears systematically, we can rewire our brains to respond to potential threats in a measured way, rather than being controlled by acute stress and panic. Before getting started conquering the fears which hold us back from our highest potential, let's explore a real case study and one of the reasons that I started writing this book in the first place.

A CASE STUDY OF FEAR AND ANXIETY

Growing up in Yorkshire and with some sporting ability, I fell in love with cricket at an early age. I can still remember the family holiday in Skegness with the small black and white portable telly on which we watched Bob Willis skittle the Aussies at Headingly. I remember the drama, the excitement, the sound of the crowd, and my Mum and Dad getting more animated than I had ever seen them. That was it: I was hooked I wanted to bowl as quick as Bob Willis and bat like "Beefy" (Ian Botham). I pestered my Dad for a real cricket bat (well, one we could use with a tennis ball) as opposed to the handmade bat he had made me which, if I am honest, was terrible. DIY isn't something that seems to have been handed down the male genetic line in my family.

Dad relented and what followed were years catching, bowling, and batting as often as I could, whenever I could. Age twelve, I was playing under thirteens, under fifteens, and under seventeens cricket for my club, Skelmanthorpe, who at the time had an amazing club team with former Pakistani and Zimbabwean International players as well as current county cricketers. Having this feast of cricket on my doorstep made my love even deeper. It was the proudest moment of my life to date when, as a thirteen-year-old, I was selected to represent Yorkshire Schoolboys.

Everything was rosey up to this point, and I had a wonderful few years in junior cricket; lots of success, plenty of failures too, but mostly positive experiences. That said, the environment was uber-competitive. I remember one of my mates being sick before a county trial (interestingly, twenty years later my mate reconnected and became a client to help him overcome anxiety around speaking in public).

EMOTIONAL RESILIENCE

My friend was not alone. Being in that environment, with the pressure I was putting on myself through heightened expectation both from myself and from others, led to me beginning to experience anxiety too. I first noticed it in the field: not wanting the ball to come to me, or praying a catch didn't come my way. Although there wasn't one precise moment that sticks out, there was an undertone of stress, a fear of failure, which was actually interfering with my enjoyment of the game. At the time, however, my sense of self was so linked with cricket that I didn't even notice that I wasn't enjoying it in the same way; it just became pervasive.

If we fast forward to me as an eighteen -year-old, I was now studying Sports Science at Loughborough University with the goal of playing first class cricket and getting a degree at the same time. I remember early on one of our lecturers saying you could do two out of three things well from a list of: your sport, your studies, and your social life—and to choose wisely.

I can honestly say I didn't make a conscious choice and instead fell into a life of drinking, socialising, and—what I didn't know at the time—anaesthetising emotion. There was a county cricket trial for Nottinghamshire during my first term which I did not turn up to through a combination of fear of failure and the belief that I wasn't good enough. At the same time as my time at University came to a close, I was witnessing some of my former compatriots and teammates pave a way into the professional game. I found that difficult and if I saw them out and about, I couldn't cope with being in their presence.

The following decade saw me progress in the Leisure and Fitness Industry, meet a wonderful woman (Jules, now my wife), play some minor counties cricket and premier league cricket in Cambridgeshire, Hampshire, and East Anglia, and crucially be introduced to personal development by James, the chairman of my cricket club at Godmanchester (Goddy) at the time. During this time, I was happy—I really was—albeit there was something missing which I could not put my finger on.

What was missing was *fulfilment* and *alignment* and the sense that I was living my *true purpose*. I was still carrying around the tag and title of being a failed sportsman around with me which felt heavy and sad. It was often how I would describe myself.

In 2008 after that initial conversation with James and subsequent conversations with Simon (my boss, at the time), it was agreed that I could attend an NLP Practitioner Course. This was back in 2008, and although I didn't notice it at the time, my life changed course forever. I realised I had never had a goal, merely a dream, that I had only ever taken small steps forwards in life that were very much within my comfort zone.

Although that pattern wasn't completely gone at the end of the week, I was much more aware and as a result committed to undertake the NLP Master Practitioner Course in 2010.

I attended the NLP Master Practitioner Course as a married man. I tied the knot with Jules in October 2009 as a result of a realisation during my first NLP week. It's amazing what happens when you take a week for yourself to work on you. I still had no intention of coaching, however, and thought that therapy was a waste of time .

After the Master course was finished, I immediately set up a coaching and therapy business with the intention to help as many people as possible to overcome imposter syndrome, fear of failure, and emotional scar-tissue keeping them stuck.

What caused the transformation?

At the end of the course, I both experienced and delivered a personal breakthrough session. This is a session whereby you and a partner both elicit a goal, and the pattern interfering with the ability to achieve that goal, before using everything you have learnt to release the negative emotions, limiting beliefs, and internal conflicts that are keeping you and your breakthrough partner stuck in different ways.

This experience was so transformational in so many ways. Firstly, I had to use everything I had learnt during the week to deliver a personal breakthrough session for Bruce, my breakthrough partner. This involved completing a full detailed personal history with my client, helping Bruce to develop a clear life-goal in all areas of life whilst helping him (and me) to see the pattern of emotional scar tissue from the past, limiting beliefs about himself, and internal conflicts which were stopping him from both moving forwards towards his goals but also stopping him feeling good day to day.

At the point of the breakthrough session, Bruce had an issue with commitment and had never had a relationship of over six months or a contract at work for more than the same period. I am not going to go into detail here for the sake of privacy, but I will say there was a lot to work with. One of the tasks pre our breakthrough session was to give to our breakthrough partner a list of Significant Emotional Events from the past a day or two before the start of the session. Bruce's "SEE" list arrived in an envelope underneath my hotel door at 10:00pm at night, the day before my breakthrough session with him, and when I read it I quietly screamed inside. He had had some of the most awful life experiences you could imagine and I felt a huge responsibility to help him heal the past and move forwards in life. I also felt terrified and for some unfathomable reason I didn't go and ask for help and support and instead committed to just doing my best.

The next day we started at 8:00am in the morning with a game to help loosen him up and relax, followed by some hypnosis to help him relax further. Once we got into the detailed personal history, things then flowed smoothly and by mid-day we could both see how his past and the emotions of anger, sadness, fear, hurt and in this case very specifically guilt, were in the way of him moving forwards towards the life he wanted but didn't believe he deserved. By 1:00pm we were completing a Time Line Therapy Session which led to Bruce healing all negative emotions associated from past events. This was huge for both of us; for Bruce, the ability to relive memories from the past which previously held such powerful negative emotions was literally liberating and emotive in a positive way. For me, without realising it at the time, I was developing the confidence in the skills I would be using over and over again to help others one-to-one and to train other therapists and coaches in.

By 5:00pm, we were releasing the belief he didn't deserve the future life he really wanted together with a number of other doubts and beliefs not in alignment with his goal. To finish the session off, we elicited his life values (priorities) and helped him to realign those values unconsciously so that going forwards he would naturally place attention on the areas of life which would help him move forwards towards his goal in balance. We finished by 7:00pm and I was exhilarated, humbled, and, to be honest, completely knackered! I slept like a baby that evening and was ready to let go and just be a client the following day. My session in comparison was much smoother and shorter in length than Bruce's albeit equally as powerful for me personally. To release the emotions of fear and disappointment in myself linked to the belief I wasn't good enough literally felt like a huge burden was lifted!

What I know for sure is that without this experience of releasing fear at that time, I would have stayed in a safe job that was beginning to lessen its appeal for me, and I would never have experienced the sense of alignment, purpose, and fulfilment which has ultimately led to me writing this book.

I have had the privilege of over the last fourteen years completing thousands of breakthrough sessions for clients one-to-one and have for the last decade training others in this methodology and love nothing more than to hear of the many breakthroughs that our associate and independent coaches and therapists deliver regularly for their clients.

SO WHAT IS FEAR AND WHY DO WE EXPERIENCE IT?

Fear is an emotion triggered by perceived danger or threat to our safety and wellbeing. When our ancient ancestors encountered life-threatening situations such as predatory animals, fear helped them react quickly to survive. The amygdala, an almond-shaped structure deep in the brain, is primarily responsible for generating fear. It constantly scans our surroundings for potential threats. When danger is detected, whether real or imagined, the amygdala instantly sends emergency signals to the nervous system to prepare for fight or flight.

This sets off a cascade of physiological changes including:

- Accelerated heart rate and breathing to circulate more oxygen to the muscles
- Release of glucose, fats, and adrenaline to supply the body with fuel and strength
- Increased sweating to cool the body
- Tunnel vision and heightened senses to zero in on the threat
- Vasoconstriction of blood vessels in extremities to maintain core blood supply

These reactions enabled our ancestors to quickly fight back or flee danger zones. However, modern day triggers of fear are often exaggerated responses to situations unlikely to cause serious harm or death. Common examples include fear of public speaking, flying, social embarrassment, darkness, injury, failure, and the unknown. While the amygdala reacts as if there is real danger, most of these threats only exist in our thoughts and imagination.

HOW FEAR AFFECTS OUR BODIES AND MINDS

When a perceived threat activates the body's stress response, hormones like adrenaline and cortisol flood the system. This triggers a wide range of effects:

PHYSICAL EFFECTS:

- Tense muscles, headaches, fatigue
- Hyperventilation, shortness of breath
- Nausea, "butterflies" in the stomach
- Insomnia, inconsistent sleep
- Lower immunity, frequent illness

MENTAL/EMOTIONAL EFFECTS:

- Racing, paranoid thoughts
- Impaired concentration and memory
- Irritability and quickness to anger
- Low motivation and avoidance
- Intense, unpleasant feelings

Left unchecked, chronic fear and anxiety can significantly damage our quality of life and even our health. Long term, the continual strain on the body from stress hormones can contribute to serious issues like heart disease, digestive problems, chronic pain, depression and burnout.

UNDERSTANDING THE ROOTS OF FEAR

Though fear originates from the ancient fight or flight response, the specific situations we find frightening stem from a blend of nature and nurture. Some fear triggers are wired in, while others are learned through life experiences. Here are a few examples of both innate and conditioned fears.

INNATE FEAR TRIGGERS:

- Loud noises: Our ancestors associated abrupt loud sounds with potential danger like predators or storms. Even babies display startle responses to noises.
- Heights: Fear of heights protected us from falls that could cause severe injury or death. Visual cues of heights like cliffs intuitively make us cautious.
- Darkness: Poor visibility at night historically increased vulnerability to unseen threats. Wariness of the dark persists even when little danger exists.
- Bugs/snakes: Small creatures that can bite/sting instinctively evoke caution. Evolution primed us to avoid potentially toxic animals.

CONDITIONED FEAR TRIGGERS:

- Trauma: Events like abuse, injury, or violence can wire the brain to see related stimuli as threats, even if no real danger exists. PTSD is an extreme example.
- Observational learning: Watching others react fearfully or suffer consequences can teach us to be afraid of the same stimuli through vicarious reinforcement.
- False information: Hearing or reading we "should" fear something like public speaking makes us anticipate anxiety before we even experience it.
- Overprotection: Being shielded from potential harm can fail to calibrate realistic vs. unrealistic fears.

Finally and perhaps most importantly is the fear of *emotion* itself. Most of the fears I have dealt with over the years have stemmed from another emotion, often embarrassment, hurt, humiliation, or disappointment bordering on sadness. When we experience these traumatic events the unconscious mind starts to try and protect us from emotional trauma the only way it knows how: the same way it keeps us safe from physical danger.

This is how my old fear of public speaking actually started, stemming from a school play and the embarrassment that went with being stood in front of an audience and having a wardrobe malfunction which led to being trouser-less on stage for a moment and the ensuing feeling of tremendous embarrassment. It was this moment that led to a period of my life where I did everything to avoid being centre of attention which was ironic as I had thrived on it as a younger child and through my sport. In order to deal with the fear of public speaking, unbeknown to me, I needed to heal *embarrassment* which when released during my 2010 breakthrough session led to me actively looking for Public Speaking Opportunities. By healing embarrassment, my unconscious mind wasn't then on the look out for the potential threat of embarrassment and as such the fear and anxiety died down to such an extent that I both actively looked for and started to enjoy speaking opportunities. We now teach Public Speaking Courses as well as provide one-to-one coaching solutions for those wanting to overcome fear and become the best version of themselves as a speaker. By the time this is published, this number maybe out of date, albeit three of the people whom we have trained in NLP have gone onto complete TEDxTalks!

IDENTIFYING FEARS

The first step in managing fear is identifying your own specific fear triggers. Ask yourself:

- What situations, places, animals or objects make me feel suddenly tense or panicky?
- Are there activities I habitually avoid out of anticipation of fear?
- Does fear hold me back from pursuing important goals? If so, if fear didn't exist what would the goal be?
- What worst case scenarios tend to play over and over in my mind? Could you imagine those events completing successfully?
- Was there a past traumatic experience, or experiences, that may have catalysed my fears?

Keeping track of fear triggers as they occur helps you detect patterns. Fears that inhibit life goals are especially important to address. Once aware of your unique "fear landscape", you can develop a tailored approach to dismantling each one.

TECHNIQUES TO OVERCOME FEAR IN THE MOMENT

When faced with an object, place, or situation that triggers fear, there are techniques to diffuse your acute stress response and stay grounded:

- Deep breathing: Inhale slowly through your nose, exhale through your mouth. Deep belly breathing

activates the parasympathetic nervous system to counter fight or flight.
- Progressive muscle relaxation: Tense and relax each muscle group to reduce tension. This also triggers relaxation response.
- Visualise a safe place: Picture somewhere you feel totally at ease. Envisioning your "happy place" helps induce tranquillity.
- Be present: Observe your surroundings using all five senses. Taking in sensory details brings focus to the present moment.
- Challenge catastrophic thinking: Ask yourself "What is the worst that could really happen?" and "How likely is it to actually happen?"
- Use the Anxiety Model: This process gets you to identify what you are anxious about and instead imagine that event completing successfully! If you remember that anxiety is always you imagining an unconscious event going badly, then you are halfway to dealing with the pattern longer term.
- Affirmations: Repeat positive phrases like "I am safe and calm" and "I can handle this." Speaking truths crowds out fearful thoughts.
- Call a friend: Describing your fear to a trusted friend can help bring rational perspective. Their reassurance can be calming.

CONQUERING FEAR LONG-TERM

While moment-to-moment management techniques help you endure periods of acute anxiety, conquering deeply ingrained fears requires continual effort to change habitual thought and behaviour patterns. Here are proven tactics:

- Gradually face fears, starting small, with mild versions of what you wish to avoid and building up towards more challenging exposures. With each successive step, the prior fear feels easier to manage. Each experience of conquering a fear weakens its power.
- Identify and challenge fearful thinking patterns when you are calm. Ask yourself questions like, "Is this thought exaggerated?", "What evidence disproves it?", and "What's a more balanced perspective?" Replace irrational fears with realistic assessments.
- Recognise fears as ultimately rooted in thoughts rather than reality. Let go of need for total certainty and control. Accept temporary discomfort as the path to growth. Have faith in your ability to handle challenges. Proudly embrace a braver identity.
- In addition to the above, getting adequate sleep, nutrition, and exercise to prevent burnout and keep stress from accumulating will also help. Make time for relaxation and fun to balance worries. Limit consumption of alarmist news that feeds anxiety.
- Where fear is concerned we can once again thoroughly recommend Time Line Therapy as a way of letting go of not only the fear as a secondary emotion but also the primary emotion, which is often sadness or hurt (sometimes shame or embarrassment—which our unconscious mind is trying to protect us from).
- Medication: Anti-anxiety medication like SSRIs can provide temporary relief while practicing other fear reduction techniques. But they are not a long term solution as they are simply dealing with the symptoms of the emotions. During acute episodes

medication can be what is required before finding a longer term solution.
- Community: Joining support groups to share advice and success stories helps build motivation. Seeing others overcome similar fears inspires us that we can too. We all face fear—you are never alone.

While lifelong phobias may feel ingrained, nearly any fear can be dismantled and in fact NLP has an ingenious way of helping clients become aware of the pattern of thought that leads to a phobic response, which often leads to clients laughing in situations they previously would have been terrified in. We have literally had clients hugging snakes in the lunch break of NLP Courses moments after a phobia intervention.

LIVING BOLDLY BY RISING ABOVE FEAR

Fear can be an obstacle, or it can be an opportunity to grow. We must shift from asking, "How can I avoid this fear?" to "How can I use this fear to become stronger?" Each time we refuse to let fear hold us back and choose to engage with life fully regardless, we build emotional resilience and boldness.

Rather than allowing the amygdala to reactively control us when potential threats arise, we can respond thoughtfully based on realistic risk. By learning to manage our fears, we prevent them from managing us. Mastering fear frees us emotionally to take risks, pursue meaningful goals, and lead vibrant, active lives aligned with our values.

The journey requires patience, persistence, and self-compassion as we retrain deeply ingrained neural pathways.

There will be ups and downs. But each small step forward builds unstoppable momentum. By boldly facing our fears, we can live life to the fullest and become the unstoppable person we were meant to be. The journey to living your best life often involves getting out of your comfort zone, embracing your fears, and then experiencing the excitement life has to offer on the other side of fear. We see this with delegates on our public speaking courses after they have conquered their fears and delivered an epic talk where they are real and authentic.

ACTIONS & REFLECTIONS FROM CHAPTER 8

Remember that those who experience the best quality of life are those who have the most comfort with uncertainty; not knowing exactly how things will pan out is precisely where the magic happens in life. What do you need to loosen the reigns of life on or with?

Live life like you are going on a personal development and healing journey. In this way, let fear be your guide on your path to self-development as you begin to get more comfortable being uncomfortable and learning from even the worst experiences.

What can you act on which you may previously have avoided doing through fear of an outcome, response or how you may feel?

CHAPTER NINE
Unravelling Hurt – A Guide to Healing

Hurt is an emotion that trails us like a shadow throughout our lives. This uninvited companion often materialises unexpectedly when someone's actions or words puncture our emotional defences. The arrow of hurt is fired when our principles or expectations clash with another's conduct, leaving us feeling wounded and violated.

The emotion of hurt is a maze. Our objective is to enhance our emotional resilience, empathy, and self-awareness when confronting the sensation of hurt so that we do not become lost.

But what precisely is hurt?

Hurt can be understood as the emotional pain we undergo when our feelings are bruised or battered. This discomfort can originate from a myriad of sources:

- The bite of insensitive or unkind words/actions from others

- Behaviour from loved ones that breaches our personal boundaries or values
- The icy jab of betrayal, rejection, or abandonment
- The anguish of loss and grief
- Unmet expectations in relationships
- The injustice of being treated unfairly or unjustly

Generally, a feeling of hurt emerges from the belief that someone else is responsible for our emotional distress. However, upon closer examination, we discover that the origin of our hurt lies not in the external world but within our own minds. Indeed, external circumstances might serve as triggers for our emotional pain, but the genesis of hurt resides in our interpretation of those events.

Consider an instance when someone's words hurt you. The same words might not impact another person in the same way. Why is that? Because our reactions are based on our unique perceptions, beliefs, values, and personal history. Our internal narrative about the event shapes our emotional response. Essentially, the cause of our hurt is not the event itself, but how we perceive and interpret it.

This realisation might feel like a bitter pill to swallow, but it holds the key to healing and emotional liberation. By shifting our focus inward and examining our responses and interpretations, we can transform our relationship with hurt. We are not merely passive recipients of hurt; we have agency and choice in how we interpret and respond to life's challenging moments.

DISSECTING HURT: CAUSES AND TRIGGERS

As previously mentioned, we often feel hurt when our personal principles or expectations collide with someone else's. This conflict becomes particularly wounding when it involves those close to us, as the discrepancy can feel like an assault on our integrity.

Let's scrutinise this further.

RELATIONSHIP VALUES:

One of the most potent sources of hurt stems from discrepancies in relationship values. Every individual brings a unique set of needs and expectations into a relationship. For instance, one partner may long for more intimacy, while the other yearns for space; one might seek open and frequent communication, while the other prefers tranquility. Similarly, variations in expectations as a result of different values can lead to misunderstandings and hurt. If you want an example of this, just think about different families' expectations around Christmas; vastly different views and opinions can cause conflict with mis-aligned expectations.

FAMILY VALUES:

Within the familial context, a common area of conflict lies around the notion of independence. Parents, often perceiving the world through a lens of experience and wisdom, might harbour different notions of independence compared to their children, who are eager to explore life on their terms. These clashing perspectives can sometimes incite feelings of hurt and misunderstanding.

SOCIAL VALUES:

In our interactions with friends or colleagues, we may encounter differences in social values. Discrepancies around principles such as ethics, punctuality, and privacy can cause misunderstandings and, subsequently, hurt.

When someone close to us behaves in a manner that conflicts with our deeply held values, it disturbs our sense of self-integrity, giving rise to feelings of hurt. Further complicating the situation, unexpressed expectations can also engender hurt when they remain unfulfilled by others. The stronger our attachment to our values and expectations, the greater the potential for hurt when these are not echoed by our loved ones.

TRACING HURT TO ITS ROOTS - PROJECTING THE PAST AND FEAR OF REJECTION

Whilst a discordance of values and expectations often serve as potent catalysts for injured feelings, these aren't the sole triggers. Traumas from past relationships and the fear of rejection and abandonment—often buried deep in our psyche—also play pivotal roles in shaping our experiences of hurt.

PROJECTING THE PAST

Visualise carrying a hefty sack of stones marked as "past hurts". Each new relationship then becomes a potential battleground, where we anticipate the recurrence of the same painful patterns. When the wounds from previous relationships remain unaddressed, they cast long, foreboding shadows onto fresh relationships. We begin to search for signs of betrayal or disappointment, often perceiving them even when they aren't present. This state of hyper-alertness places a strain on new relationships, establishing barriers to genuine intimacy. The key to shattering this relentless cycle is to confront and heal past hurts. By permitting ourselves to grieve and engage in self-work, we can release these burdensome stones and open ourselves to healthier relational dynamics.

REJECTION AND ABANDONMENT

Encountering rejection or abandonment can create severe emotional pain. Our fundamental need to feel valued, accepted, and secure in relationships makes the withdrawal of presence or affection by loved ones profoundly hurtful. The sting of rejection undermines our core attachment needs, sending waves of hurt rippling through our emotional terrain. Fostering inner security and self-love can act as a buffer, mitigating the intensity of hurt when relationships inevitably fluctuate or dissolve.

NAVIGATING THROUGH HURT

Our instinctive response to hurt is often to lay blame at the feet of the individual who ignited it, to cloak our wounds in anger and defence mechanisms. Yet, a path of greater wisdom invites us to process hurt in ways that foster understanding (both of ourselves and others), personal growth, and emotional resilience.

In the following sections, we will sketch out some constructive strategies to handle hurt more effectively. Our objective is to transform our relationship with hurt from unwelcome visitor into a stern yet enlightening mentor. Through this transformation, we can fortify our emotional resilience and deepen our understanding of ourselves and our relationships.

REFLECT ON WHAT THE HURT SIGNIFIES

When you're enveloped by hurt, take a moment to retreat and explore what it is disclosing about you. Ask yourself: What personal values or expectations have been violated? Which unhealed wounds could be dictating my reactions? By viewing hurt as an internal summons for comprehension, we can garner valuable insights about our values, needs, and areas ripe for growth.

COMMUNICATE WITH COMPASSION

Communication is an important tool in the healing process. When you feel ready to speak to the person who has triggered your emotional hurt response, articulate your feelings honestly, ensuring your words are empathetic. If speaking to them directly is too much, you could try journalling first. Endeavour to comprehend the other person's standpoint. Bear in mind, the goal isn't to launch an attack, but to foster understanding and restoration. In time you may even be able to take ownership of how you are feeling and frame it in a way in which makes the other person aware that you know that how you are feeling isn't their fault it is just that it triggered you.

CHANNEL ANGER CONSTRUCTIVELY

Anger often forms a defensive shell over our hurt, signalling that something dear to us has been threatened. It's crucial to direct this anger in a productive manner. Engage in peaceful activities like exercise, meditation, or creative pursuits to aid in dissipating the accumulated energy. Unaddressed anger can brew and manifest destructively, making it vital to find a healthy avenue for its expression. If you find yourself story-telling mentally, creating more anger, it becomes even more important to dissipate the emotion before addressing any issues.

EXTEND FORGIVENESS TO OTHERS AND YOURSELF

In the intricate dance of relationships, missteps are inevitable. Extending forgiveness to others, and importantly, to ourselves, is a pivotal step in the healing journey. Forgiveness doesn't translate to forgetting or endorsing harmful actions. Rather, it signifies making peace with the past and liberating ourselves to progress without the weight of unresolved grievances.

GRIEF AND LOSS

As we have touched on in earlier chapters, loss can be a profound source of hurt. Give yourself permission to fully experience and process grief when a relationship concludes or when someone you love passes away. Emotional catharsis can be achieved through crying, journaling, or engaging in heartfelt conversations with others who might relate to what you are going through. Remember, grieving is a critical part of the healing journey, and it unfolds at its own pace.

LEARN AND GROW

Recovering from hurt isn't merely about assuaging pain, it's also about evolving from the experience. Identify the lessons gleaned, establish healthy boundaries, and broaden your emotional awareness. By doing so, you transform the painful encounter with hurt into a catalyst for personal growth and emotional resilience.

With consistent practice, we can become proficient at detecting the onset of hurt, consciously processing it, and responding from a place of emotional maturity. Welcoming hurt as merely another facet in the diamond of our lives allows us to not only survive it, but emerge more robust, enlightened, and resilient.

CHAPTER TEN

Overcoming Guilt and Regret

Guilt is an emotion that lingers in our hearts and minds, acting as a weight that can both guide us to self-knowledge and pull us down. Picture it as a warning bell, alerting us when our actions don't align with our inner values. But what happens when this alarm rings too loudly, too often, or unnecessarily? Most of us experience guilt even when it is not justified. This can interfere with us taking time and looking after ourselves; it can warp our relationships with others; and perhaps most insidiously, it can distort our intentions. When we act out of guilt rather than genuine motivation to do something, our action is much less likely to be effective. In short, rampant guilt undermines emotional resilience.

UNDERSTANDING GUILT

Guilt seems to be in the very DNA of the human race. Indeed, the biblical story of Adam and Eve traces guilt (and its cousin blame) back to the very first human beings to walk the Earth. Adam and Eve are given a clear moral imperative, and when they break that imperative, they feel a sudden sense of shame and self-awareness, one that causes Adam to hide from God for the first time. Adam also blames Eve for the error, even though he is fully aware of the consequences of his actions and in control when he decides to also taste of the forbidden fruit. Likewise, when we feel intense guilt, we often resort to passing the blame onto a person, organisation, or power beyond us to soothe our sense of self-loathing.

Whether we view the story of Adam and Eve figuratively, literally, or otherwise, there is a wisdom in acknowledging how deeply ingrained guilt can be in the way we think and feel, whilst also recognising how harmful and often unnecessary an emotion it is.

That said guilt can, of course, serve positive purposes. When guilt alerts us to genuine wrongdoing, it can steer us to make amends or adjust our future behaviour.

But of course, guilt often gets out of hand, becoming a shadow that grows when fed by unrealistic expectations, perfectionism, and a distorted sense of responsibility. When our burden of guilt becomes too heavy—the shadow too vast—we become vulnerable to self-doubt, regret, and feelings of inadequacy.

PATHWAYS TO PROBLEMATIC GUILT

When does guilt overstep its bounds?

Crossing a Moral Line: Think of a time when your actions felt at odds with your beliefs. The aftermath of this internal battle can leave you constantly going over the past and regretting your decisions.

Chasing Perfection: Have you ever chased an unattainable ideal, only to be met with disappointment and guilt at your failure to achieve it? The pursuit of impossible goals transforms the healthy ambition of excellence into a relentless cycle of self-criticism.

Shouldering the World: Sometimes, we carry the weight of responsibility even for things beyond our control. This burdensome guilt can be both confusing and undeserved and we find this feeling is often pervasive within the family environment and, even worse, reinforced by well-meaning family members trying to pass on their own moral values.

The Echo of Childhood: Reflect on the lessons of right and wrong from your early years. How has strict or inconsistent parenting shaped your perception of guilt? Can you think of memories from the distant past that, when you re-live them now, still create the feeling of guilt internally? If so, this is a sign that your past conditioning is interfering with your present experiences of life. Don't worry there are things you can do to let go of the past and to move on.

The Voices of Society and Culture: Consider the influences around you - from religion to social media. How have they moulded your sense of guilt? Many people's sense of religion is of a higher power which is judgemental of wrong doing and yet if you read any of the sacred texts from all religions they talk of a higher power which is beyond right and wrong, judgement and righteousness and instead the references are of an ultimately forgiving, kind, loving presence which permeates everything.

Guilt often manifests as continuously blaming oneself without seeing the whole picture. Over time, this pattern can pull one's mental health down. After all, we are all just doing the best we can at the time. Appreciating this simple fact is one of the best ways to let challenging life events and imperfections to pass.

PARENTING

Virtually all parents hold the irrational fear of damaging their children emotionally. As I went on a personal development journey, this fear actually got *worse* for me initially, rather than better. In realising the sheer extent of the scar tissue I had to work through from my childhood, I started to fear messing my own kids up. However, scar tissue is inevitable. The best we can do is be the best version of ourself and help our children to navigate their own scar tissue as best they can. We can't control the education system, their friend, or their hobbies, we can just be an ever present source of support for them and do our best knowing we will never get it exactly right and that they also don't expect us to!

PERFECTIONISM

I spoke recently with a young man who is an excellent rugby player with the passion, the talent, and the desire to go on to make a professional career out of his sport. The problem, however, was that the heightened expectations he was now experiencing—and the strong desire to please others—were making the job of playing at his best almost impossible.

The fear of failure would then become a catalyst for poor performance, which in turn would cause him to feel tremendous guilt. *All these people believe in me and have invested in me and I am letting them down.* Of course, the guilt only reinforced the fear of failure, thus creating a vicious cycle.

For clarity's sake, let's draw a line between fear of failure and guilt, which is perhaps easier to see in family relationships where there is a desire to please. We want to please and fear failing and letting someone down. If we fear failure, it makes failure more likely (we get what we focus on) and then guilt is triggered as we have now manifested precisely what we don't want: the perception of letting someone down (which we now feel guilty about).

He has a journey ahead of him where he needs to learn to be kind to himself in his reviews of his performance, and focus on what he can learn from each experience rather than what went wrong. This sounds simple, but I know from personal experience how difficult it can be to re-write those narratives. It involves working with an inner game coach to let go of limiting beliefs such as "If it's not perfect, it's not good enough" and "I am a failure!" He has half the battle won: he has the talent and the passion. What's next is to learn a healthy, high performance mindset, a new "virtuous" cycle of setting high intentions whilst letting go of the outcome and learning from whatever the experience is.

RELATIONSHIPS

Fear of loss, or fear of being hurt, often gets in the way of truly being ourselves in relationships, and can often mean that we fail to communicate about our true wants and needs.

We all have a complex mix of introverted and extroverted energy in relationships, and that means that we all need different amounts of time with others and by ourselves. Add into this that, to be healthy, we also need time in nature and time with silence or minimal distraction (that many of us aren't actually allowing ourselves) and we can see just how challenging it can be for a relationship to work.

Many people experience intense guilt when they think of taking time for themselves. They worry that they are insulting their partner by wanting time alone. But without that time for reflection—which is a basic need we often don't acknowledge—we will not be able to show up in the relationship as our best self. Relationships are another example of fear and guilt working hand in hand to stymie the blossoming of a positive thing in our lives. Fear of disappointing or offending our partner reinforces the guilt of asking for what we need. We need to replace this guilt with honest dialogue about what we need as individuals to be healthy, and then we must support our partner to take that time for themselves as well. We must overcome societal conditioning ,which posits "You have to put others first". Putting others first is great if you are looking after yourself well. In fact, there is nothing more satisfying! However many people are literally trying to give from an empty vessel and in turn they end up cracking or having an emotional episode as a result with the aftermath often being —you guessed it—guilt!

It's become a common analogy to use: when you are on an airplane, they tell you to always put your own oxygen mask on first before trying to help someone else.

But though many of us know we need to put our oxygen mask on first, few of us actually do this in practice. Usually, this is because guilt keeps interfering with the process. As we go to apply our oxygen mask, guilt chastises us for thinking selfishly. Over time, we become less and less able to show up for others as deprivation of care weakens us. Guilt, therefore, erodes our emotional resilience.

Guilt can grow larger than life, weighing heavily on our hearts and minds, threatening to overwhelm us. The longer we hold off putting on our oxygen mask, the more at risk of burn-out we become.

Let's examine some practical strategies for dealing with guilt.

THE PATH TO AWARENESS

Regularly pause and reflect, assessing if guilt is subtly or not-so-subtly effecting or interfering with your quality of life or the ability to either look after yourself and do what is right for you!

A BALANCED PERSPECTIVE

Study the situation with clear eyes, even seeking a trusted friend or partner's perspective, as long as it doesn't involve them.

Match your guilt with the context: whose responsibility is it truly? Can you let go of some of this guilt consciously?

CREATING A HIGH PERFORMANCE PRACTICE

Transform a perceived failure into a lesson, a step on your life's journey.

Focus on growth, seeing each stumble as a chance to rise stronger.

MINDFULNESS

Engage in mindfulness and / or meditation, a gentle anchor to the present.

Free yourself from the bonds of past mistakes, focusing on the present through exploring breath-work.

SELF-CARE

Embrace activities in nature that nourish your soul and body.

Enhance your emotional well-being by exploring issues with a coach or therapist to dig deep to uncover and heal the roots of guilt.

SELF-FORGIVENESS

Speak to yourself as you would your child, understanding that to err is human.

Cultivate self-love and acceptance, forgiving yourself as you would forgive a child; remember, whatever our age, we are always doing the best we can with what we have at the time.

If the feeling of guilt is particularly deep-seated or "heavy", then seek to make amends where needed, aligning actions with your core values. Feel free to apologise and don't expect anything in return; it is the act itself which is the gift.

By living more and more truly to yourself, and recognising and honouring your responsibilities, you will slowly be able to shed the leaden mantle of guilt and breathe the free air again.

EMOTIONAL RESILIENCE

Finally, for those still convinced that being hard on yourself is the path to achievement ,consider the following: anxiety is often a signal of being hard on yourself. Anxiety, in other words, can be deeply intertwined with guilt.

∼

LET me give an example from my work with a top-50 rated golfer in the world.

Early on in our journey, before he hit these dizzying heights, we worked on his fear of missing short putts and the anxiety created by his pattern of being hard on himself if he did miss. The anxiety was caused by the unconscious mind working to try and protect him from a perceived threat (his own emotional reaction to missing). By learning to accept the outcome of any golf shot including a short putt, he was able to, in time, feel comfortable over the ball without the anxiety he previously experienced.

Let's look at a slightly heavier example too.

People who have been abused are statistically more likely to abuse themselves; the guilt is heavy and actually makes it more likely to re-create those circumstances and the guilt itself. Like attracts like.

One more example to make the point: why do marketeers label food as naughty and nice? Because they understand the ego and the pattern of the ego wanting to feel pleasure and pain (the guilt or regret from the perceived naughty food). We'll go deeper into this in our chapter on compulsion!

Have you ever felt a nervousness/bordering on excitement at doing something which you may feel guilty about at a later date, teenage years come to mind for me when experimenting or stretching boundaries.

How these situations are handled as parents is crucial, being too harsh can result on a compulsion to rebel. Non intervention can lead to a normalisation of behaviours and situations that maybe are not appropriate. Parenting is challenging for so many reasons and parental guilt and anxiety is itself so common! As already mentioned, when I first learnt NLP before becoming a dad, I felt terrified of all the things we could do wrong and the damage we could do! In time, however, my attitude has completely changed to this, as parents we are going to make mistakes and our children will have times of suffering. It is in these moments that the seeds of personal development occur. So, as a parent now, I want my children to have as comfortable and enjoyable childhood as possible, albeit my response to challenges is more grounded as it is these challenges that will provide both of them (no plans for a third) with the opportunity to grow and evolve. Of course, this is ultimately their responsibility; we can only guide and provide opportunities for reflection.

With greater awareness we can see situations more clearly and become able to reflect on past experiences differently in order to move past anxiety without acting upon it. As we develop our journey of awareness, we can see the interplay of emotions and how we can choose to react differently in order to live a life of greater ease and enjoyment both in our own lives and with our direct responsibilities for others.

CHAPTER ELEVEN

Humiliation, Shame, & Embarrassment

When I originally scoped out this book, this chapter was missing. However, over the four to five years it has taken to bring this work into fruition, the number of clients I have worked with suffering from the effect of these emotions has made this an essential component to include.

∾

So, what bearing do humiliation, shame, and embarrassment have on emotional resilience? Well, to be truly resilient we need to be able to approach situations we may previously have avoided and, as we have explored in previous chapters, guilt and fear often stops us from enjoying experiences and performing at our best. What I have found is that often tangled in the root of fear and guilt are the emotions we label as humiliation, shame, and embarrassment.

We all code and give meaning to our experiences and use different words to describe how we feel, so what one person deems embarrassing another finds shameful or humiliating. In essence, therefore, we are actually talking about the same experience: an external event or trigger makes us feel deeply, deeply uncomfortable. We have all experienced these moments where we want the world to swallow us up and, as unusual as this may seem, I would like you now to spend some time reflecting on those moments. I recognise that reliving these moments, even in memory, can be extraordinarily difficult. But sometimes we have to face things head on in order for them to get better, and to weaken the power they hold over us.

By reflecting and journalling those emotions, you may be able to see where fear has then entered your life (usually to try and avoid experiencing those emotions again).

So, hard as this may be, please take some time to write down your worst five instances of shame, humiliation, embarrassment....

Now that you have brought these emotional experiences into more conscious awareness, to what extent do you still feel that emotion when you relive those memories? How strong is the emotion out of ten when you relive that memory mentally now?

For some, a lot of embarrassment can often be felt during our socialisation phase, between the ages of fourteen to twenty-one, and continuing into our early twenties. During this time, we undergo significant programming and feel societal pressure to fit in. Though this continues into adulthood, we are often better equipped to handle it, though not always, hence the addition of this chapter!

I remember as a student at Loughborough University I was a sports billy, studying sports science. I loved sport: watching, playing, and competing. And yet, when asked if I wanted to play hall sports such as basketball, hockey, or volleyball, I repeatedly said no! I remember the discomfort I had in saying no as I really wanted to; so why go against something which was innately in me? The answer is I wanted to fit in. I had slotted into a peer group of hard drinking northerners (life is amazing when you think back). They were all good sportsmen in their own right playing their own sports to a high level albeit seemingly unhappy to play sport at a more collegiate, friendly level (or maybe they too were projecting what they thought others would think). We will never know, but what I can say is that I regretted missing out on those opportunities to take part in other sports, meet new people, and enjoy the sheer fun of taking part in sport without any perceived expectations.

At that stage of my life, cricket was my life and my plan was to become a professional county cricketer.

About the same time that I was making these decisions to not partake in hall sport, I was also making other decisions which could and indeed did have more wide reaching consequences for my life. Twelve weeks into my first term as a first year undergraduate at Loughborough I had a trial for Nottinghamshire County Cricket Club at Loughborough University itself. This was as a result of a very successful year playing for Yorkshire U19s the year before. I had earned the opportunity, yet as time went on I felt less and less comfortable with the upcoming trial. I was training with Loughborough University and was in awe at some of the talent on show and so I decided not to tell anyone, I kept it a secret; I didn't want to make a show or to be seen to be a big fish. As this narrative took hold in my inner dialogue, I started to both fear failure at the trial itself as well as perceived embarrassment and judgement of others.

So what did I do? Well, without anyone to discuss this with, I chose what seemed like the most sensible option, at least to my young immature mind: I followed my uncomfortable emotions of fear and quite simply didn't turn up, without telling anyone about my decision.

The emotional impact of this decision hit me later as I witnessed friends of mine successfully follow their dreams of becoming professional cricketers, knowing that I hadn't even given my dreams a chance. By wanting to avoid embarrassment, and by following the voice of fear, I ended up with a deep sense of sadness and regret which— not knowing any better—I buried.

Now, may years later, I am grateful for these experiences as they are what led me to personal development and to where I am now. In my twenties, however, they were experiences I buried without reflection, avoiding any discomfort that went with that.

ACTIONS & REFLECTIONS FROM CHAPTER 11

Consider the following:

- How have past embarrassments shaped your life?
- Where in life do you avoid the judgement of others?
- What would you do differently if you felt you were truly able to choose what you would really like to do for you?
- If past embarrassments & humiliations had no weight for you what would you do that you are not currently doing?

CHAPTER TWELVE

Compulsion, Addiction & Emotion Cycles

At first glance, compulsion and addiction sounds like something serious, something only relevant to those who end up in rehab, yet if we are honest with ourselves very few live a life that isn't in some way affected by compulsive patterns (which are essentially patterns of thought, emotion, and energy).

RESPONDING NOT CHOOSING

When we talk about compulsion specifically, we aren't necessarily just talking about drug or alcohol abuse, although this can be the case. We are certainly referring to moments where you feel compelled to act or re-act in a certain way.

For example, this could be the compulsion to eat sugary food at a certain time of day.

It could be a compulsion to react in a specific way to a certain person, situation, or even word.

It could also be a behavioural compulsion, such as having to exercise constantly, or cleaning, or checking our phone.

When we really interrogate ourselves and our motivations, we often find we are not truly "choosing" our behaviours, but simply responding unconsciously to stimuli.

Do we really need to eat the doughnut to feel good about ourselves?

Do we need to make a snarky comment to our spouse to protect ourselves or could we be vulnerable for a change?

Do we need to look at our phone the moment we wake up, or can we just be with our feelings in that moment and create a different more mindful morning routine?

Now, having reflected on this, what areas of life do you demonstrate compulsive tendencies?

Take a pen and paper out or electronic notebook and take five minutes to list your own compulsive tendencies…

WHAT DRIVES COMPULSION?

Now that we have a degree of awareness around compulsive tendencies, let's look a little bit more closely at what compulsive tendencies actually are.

A compulsion, in essence, is where you are strongly pulled towards some form of activity or behaviour. Therefore, there is a motivation or a drive to behave in a certain way.

This motivation or drive is fuelled by an emotion, typically either anger, guilt, frustration, fear, anxiety, or very occasionally sadness and hurt. Sadness and hurt tend to be the deeper scars and the other emotions kick in in order to try and prevent us experiencing the deeper pain of hurt or sadness.

This can be clearly seen in eating disorders and compulsions, where the food is often the solution to filling the void of emptiness, loneliness, or sadness. Be honest, who hasn't noticed a change in their eating and exercise pattern — either positively or negatively — post a relationship breakdown or loss of a loved one.

It could be argued that all addictive and compulsive patterns are linked to a sense of lack of fulfilment and purpose.

People who are deeply fulfilled in their life are very unlikely to be experiencing the same kind of addictive patterns, as they are not trying to use external stimuli to lay over the top of the lack of fulfilment that many others are experiencing. But becoming fulfilled is not easy. Recent stats showed that engagement levels (meaning the extent to which people found their work fulfilling and were committed to it) in the UK, United States, and Europe are *incredibly* low. The majority of people are unfulfilled at work. Divorce rates are at an all-time-high too, which likely indicates people are not fulfilled in their relationships either.

So, how do we address this major issue?

Putting aside the global and national scale for now, which we address extensively in my other book *Mapping Motivation for Coaching* written with James Sale, the creator of Motivational Maps, let's return to looking at the individual.

When tackling an addictive or compulsive pattern as a coach, one has to look more deeply at the underlying condition as opposed to the symptom being presented.

Emotional patterns are fuelled by unconscious thoughts and the essence of unconsciousness is that you feel the discomfort and those emotional feelings drive your behaviour without conscious awareness of the specific sequence of thought which is creating the emotional discomfort and the behaviour in the first place.

One of the solutions, therefore, to unpicking compulsion is to endeavour to become aware of the pattern itself. At a basic level, becoming aware of any negative trait can lead to a change in behaviour, as we are able to make conscious choices in an area of previous unconsciousness.

This, in essence, is the feedback loop which we receive throughout our lives. We are consistently receiving feedback from our environment and our loved ones and those work colleagues we admire. Responding to that feedback, and learning to behave in a different way in response to that old stimulus, will eventually create new habits. This is a well-worn, much-accepted path we have all taken from time-to-time, and because compulsions are learnt behaviour they can of course be unlearnt when the source of the behaviour and the unconscious patterns are acknowledged and recognised.

Saying all of this, awareness alone is not enough. You have to maintain awareness and programme new habits which typically take 12 weeks to embed so you have to be willing to act. In the early stages of re-writing a behavioural pattern, this can be excruciating, as it takes far more energy to carve a new path than to follow the furrow of an old one. The brain is an efficient machine. It establishes pathways and then expects us to keep using them. Forging a new path is harder, at first, but gets easier with each new repetition. This is why I ask clients to celebrate mini-wins where they make a different choice to the unconscious habit, these moments are magic as it shows our ability to make changes consciously despite our unconscious programming.

In NLP we often talk about "Who is driving the bus" meaning who is the person whom is aware of the old programming and the patterns, this of course is the real us our seat of awareness, our consciousness. This awareness itself is life changing as we realise we are not our old patterns we are the awareness of those patterns and everything else!

The good news is, feedback can raise your levels of awareness and move past and beyond those patterns as opposed to trying to resist them and overcome those patterns through willpower.

To raise awareness, therefore, let's begin to look at some typical emotional patterns which lead to compulsive behaviour.

ANGER AND GUILT AND THEIR ROLE IN RELATIONSHIPS

Who here hasn't, as a parent, partner, colleague, or loved one, reacted angrily to a certain word, only then to find themselves feeling incredibly guilty shortly thereafter?

Whether the pattern of anger and guilt is a well worn trench, or just a lightly trodden path, the solution to this triggered reaction is the same. Firstly, we have to learn to be forgiving and accepting of our initial reaction. This is often a surprise to therapeutic clients because the nature of egoic patterns is the addiction to pleasure *and* pain which of course is the opposite of peace and contentment. If you like: the nature of addiction is the experience of highs and lows rather than the more even and balanced experience of deeper peace, contentment, and enlightenment. The latter is far healthier for us, but of course we are all drawn to the rollercoaster ride of the highs and lows.

As a result, in order to reduce our compulsion to be angry, for example, we need to convince ourselves we will be kind in the eventuality that we make a mistake. This circumnavigates the addiction to the highs and lows. Remember, as strange as it may sound, when we are trapped in the cycle of addiction, we are enjoying the lows as much as the high. But if we avoid the low—the self-criticism, the judgement, the blame, the self-loathing—then we begin to short circuit the desire for the high.

We must be consistent, however, because our ego loves nothing more than to beat ourselves up for the behaviour that we've just demonstrated.

There are similarities between this pattern and others, and learning to be forgiving of whatever behaviour you have demonstrated in the past is a hugely significant step towards letting go of addictive and/or compulsive behaviour.

Think about it for a minute: if you were able to fully accept whatever the outcome of a job interview was, you'd probably feel less nervous about showing up. And this relaxation would ironically probably mean a better performance in the interview! Addiction is similar. If you are no longer afraid of the consequences of "failing" to resist a certain urge, because you are able to love yourself no matter what, then the terrible stress and strain of "resisting" the compulsion is alleviated, which gives you more energy, more focus, more resolve. The self-criticism that often comes with "succumbing" to an addictive urge only batters you down further, weakening resolve, and deepening the hold the addiction or compulsion has over you.

You can apply this thinking to exams, work opportunities, relationships, and any other context.

So, as well as practicing forgiveness, we must also let go of the outcome; this is especially the case in emotional patterns where fear and anxiety crop up, because fear and anxiety are heightened when we anticipate how we will react ourselves to the disappointment or frustration of things not going our way.

Let's look at another example where emotions can cycle around food, which is a big area of challenge for so many people.

CHEESECAKE!

One of my clients had a pattern of overeating: not only eating too big portions but always clearing everything which was on his plate. This was clearly a pattern learnt from childhood where he was taught the importance of eating everything on a plate so that things did not go to waste. Many people with war-generation parents, who experienced rationing, will relate to having this mentality inflicted upon them during childhood. His pattern was exacerbated by his wife's pattern of demonstrating love through cooking and providing big meals.

In order to solve this problem, which had been going on for ten to fifteen years and had led to significant weight gain, he needed to become aware of the pattern and the beliefs and emotions surrounding them. This was absolutely an addictive, compulsive cycle where he would feel guilty if he didn't finish everything that was on his plate—and not just the plate, but any portion of food whether that be a pack of doughnuts, a pack of sweets, or a bowl of fruit.

By becoming aware of the pattern, he was able to discuss it with his wife and elicit her help to develop strategies to deal with the situation in a different way, without either of them becoming hurt or negatively triggered by sudden change of outlook or behaviour.

Let's have a little look at the emotions involved with eating compulsions. To do so, we will have to understand the ego at a deeper level.

When we talk about the ego in personal development circles, we don't just refer to brash or arrogant behaviour which is what most people associate with this word. Instead, we refer to any pattern of conditioned thought or emotion that makes us feel uncomfortable or react negatively out of that discomfort.

To demonstrate this, it's useful to think of the ego as that part of our conditioning that likes nothing more than to experience the highs and lows of pleasure and pain. In the words, the ego is in essence *addicted* to pain and pleasure, whereas our higher self enjoys nothing more than peace and contentment and doesn't need anything outside of itself to be at peace.

If you prefer to think of these concepts in more psychological terms, then think of your higher self as the part of you that is aware and watching at all times—therefore, is above or "higher" than the part of you that is directly involved in what is transpiring. Consider this: if you have too much to drink, there is still a part of you that is aware you are drunk! Even though your mental faculties have been compromised, there is a part of you that is "higher" than merely intellectual processing, and can register the fact that you are in a compromised state. This is one of the great miracles of being a sentient being. All parents have at some point felt anger towards their children and yet not acted angrily and there is that miracle in action again!

To return to the ego, it loves the guilt and the beating ourselves up period post overeating just as much as the eating! We have been taught to label certain foods as "naughty". Far from putting us off, this turns us on even more. If you think of other habits: sex, drugs, alcohol, you will see that their potential taboo only further incentivises us to engage with them. There is a reason why marketeers promote certain foods as "naughty but nice"; they understand the ego enjoys the seesaw between pleasure and pain. Therefore, in order to overcome this pattern, it is a surprise for many clients that the solution is not to use willpower but instead to forgive themselves for whatever action they take and whatever they eat.

If they can learn to enjoy the meal without any guilt, there will be less compulsion, in the same way that the pro golfer learned to accept the outcome of any putt—and anxiety associated with the outcome first lessened and then disappeared.

By learning to be forgiving and accepting of whatever you eat, and thereby removing guilt, the compulsion to eat something labelled as "naughty" will diminish. It is also really wise to drop the label of naughty; it isn't naughty food, it is just food!

The emotional pattern, or cycle, with food can often look something like this.

1. Sadness, boredom, or lack of fulfilment leading to the desire for distraction
2. The desire for distraction leads to a thought about a certain food type
3. The thought about the food type leads to a feeling of excitement or compulsion to eat
4. This compulsion leads to very rapid or quick eating, unconscious eating, if you like, followed by deep remorse or guilt.

This pattern, of course, is the same across virtually all addictions.

One of my clients had an addiction to cheesecake. It's not the most serious of addictions, and as a result is a good example, as we can take the learnings and apply them to our own patterns without it getting too heavy.

After our first session, I set the client the task of buying a cheesecake and setting the cheesecake down in front of her on the table. The task was to sit still with the cheesecake for as long as possible without eating it. The immediate response was, "I can't! I will eat it!" To which I replied, "Yes, I know. However, before you do, I want you to write down the emotions you are feeling, where are they in the body, and what thoughts you are aware of."

This task helps the client to momentarily act out of the higher self, that place of awareness all human beings possess where we are aware of our emotions as opposed to being a slave to them. Inevitably, the client did eat the cheesecake but not before becoming aware of a pattern of sadness, emptiness, frustration and guilt which she felt in her stomach and chest.

The second element to this task was for the client to enjoy the cheesecake and to slow down and really savour every mouthful, and funnily enough this was the part of the task which the client found most difficult, as she was working against the unconscious pull to eat really quickly. By doing so, she became aware of the desire to get the experience over with as quickly as possible so she could get to the part where she could reprimand herself and beat herself up for what had just transpired. Again, we are just as addicted to the guilt, shame, and remorse as we are to the thing itself.

The third element of the task was for the client to immediately forgive herself for eating the cheesecake and to fully accept what had just happened and to be kind to herself and this element of the task the client considered a complete failure. However, in truth, she came back to the next session with a heightened awareness of the feelings of worthlessness and of not being good enough. All of the patterns which you become aware of, you can let go of, whereas those that remain unconscious persist!

As so often is the case, the cheesecake was symbolic for something much deeper. We were able to set about working to release the sadness from past events, the trauma from the past, and the other negative emotions and beliefs about herself which she was now aware of. In time, the cheesecake stopped being a thing.

ACTIONS & REFLECTIONS FROM CHAPTER 12

Consider what compulsions do you have? Allow yourself a moment of honesty in your reflections.

What behaviours or actions do you hold guilt or shame around? Acknowledgement of this is to is the first step to overcoming the pattern.

Once you have acknowledged your compulsions the next stage is to forgive yourself completely for the past. After all forgiveness is the process of stopping pretending that the past could have been any different, and remember you have always being doing the best you can with what you have and the level of awareness you have been operating at until this point.

What do you need to forgive yourself for?

It may well be worth looking for a coach/therapist to support your journey in this area and please don't underestimate the power of first acknowledging and opening up to yourself and then someone else in this space.

CHAPTER THIRTEEN

Overcoming Emotional Attachments

I think everyone can relate to some form of emotional attachment at some point within their lives. In previous chapters, we have discussed the sadness and grief that can be experienced with the loss of loved ones, and how we can be afraid of letting that grief go. In this chapter, we will explore other forms of emotional attachments which range from the strength of an emotional attachment to a partner through to the attachment to an animal, a house, a job or title, or an object we have within our possession.

Being in the UK post-pandemic was challenging for many and with cost of living high for many people up and down the country, many are becoming aware of emotional attachments which we may previously have been completely unaware of. For example, the attachment to our ability to socialise, exercise, participate in sport, eat out at a nice restaurant. And of course, it's not just what these things are but what they *represent* that we are attached to.

Our intention in this chapter is to both bring these areas to our conscious awareness and provide practical advice of what you can do to move through, past, and beyond attachments that are no longer serving you, so that you can live life with greater peace ease and fulfilment…

To begin with, let me share a recent personal experience which shines a light on some of the subtler emotional attachments and how they can play into some of the deeper emotions under the surface.

The last ten years have been the happiest and most fulfilled of my life so far, and they coincide with the set up of our business in 2010, the move into our new home, and the birth of our two children Aidan (in 2011) and Ellie (in 2014). Just prior to moving house (move number two) in February 2021, I woke up in the night having what I could only describe as a panic attack.

I had never experienced an episode like this; it took me absolutely by surprise. I felt searing pain and anxiety, and the trigger appeared to be the impending house move—at least that's how it felt.

I explained my feelings to my wife that morning who was obviously concerned and worried not only for me but the family (and to be fair, everyone in the "house chain"). It was imperative that I found some peace with the move as we were (thankfully) both aware enough and far enough down our personal development journey to know that sabotaging the move through listening to the anxious thinking was not the right course.

As a result, we both agreed I should get an emergency coaching session booked in ASAP. I am so grateful to have such an amazing network of people around me—which made this highly possible! The following day I had a zoom call with my coach and fifteen minutes in he asked me,

"Bevis, what do you need to let go of to be comfortable with the house move?"

The answer was "My Mum."

Queue floods of tears, a moment of release, and the subsequent peace of mind both about the move but also another key moment in my grieving process. Looking back now, I can see that I raised my family in that house and symbolically there was an attachment between that house, my happiness, and the happiness of my family (which included my Mum). The discomfort I experienced was ultimately a signpost to greater awareness and, with coaching, allowed me to take another much needed step on the grieving path.

I hope the example above gives you an insight into how seemingly mundane emotional attachments can be linked to deeper ones, and provide food for thought to consider what webs of attachment may exist in your own life.

THERAPEUTIC DETACHMENT

Therapists use detachment as a way of helping their clients to gain perspective on events, to access a non-emotional state where the facts can be reviewed clearly. In Timeline Therapy, we use detachment to help our clients let go of all emotion from all previous events that the client is aware of.

Detachment is a useful tool for therapy but it is also something else. Spiritual leaders talk of detachment in terms of becoming aware of your true nature as a human being. By becoming aware of your essence , your core, your true self, your spirit, you discover that you are pure awareness. By growing this awareness of your true essential nature, you become less attached to material things, people, circumstances, events, places, careers, houses, cars and all the rest.

At its zenith, living a detached or unattached life means that ultimately any event could occur in your life and you would be okay with that event occurring due to your awareness of your essential nature.

Detachment therefore has clear and obvious links to emotional resilience and in this segment we'll explore both the detachment used for therapeutic purposes and becoming more emotionally resilient as well as the reverse of detachment: inhabiting our body, thoughts, and emotions where and when it is appropriate to do so. This way, we can learn how to be present and use knowledge of association and dissociation to create greater resilience...

Most people I speak to have at some point experienced being woken up in the night by an emotion linked to a recent event which they are now playing over and over in their mind.

If this is something you recognise, or which resonates with you, try an alternative approach.

It is the *emotion* that is keeping you awake — not the event. Past events have emotions stored within them. Often, there is still something for us to learn from these events. Assuming this memory isn't a major trauma, more like something frustrating or annoying or worrying, then have a go at the following process.

Instead of reliving that event and therefore re-experiencing the emotion, as you see the person or situation or problem, aim to re-experience that memory from a detached perspective with you seeing yourself in the picture from a bird's eye view. If you've ever played a video-game, it might help you to imagine you are watching the event unfold from a third person perspective.

Now you are detached and seeing yourself in the picture, this is what in NLP we called "disassociation". Notice the difference in how you feel. The more you disassociate, the further away you draw that bird's eye perspective, the more emotion disappears completely until there may even be no emotion whatsoever.

Once you have mastered this, you've taken a big step towards gaining greater emotional resilience, being able to disassociate or detach from a painful memory at will. Now, rather than being kept up all night, you can disassociate and detach and then ask yourself what it is you need to learn from this event. The learning will allow you to let go of the emotion.

In NLP and Timeline Therapy we believe that emotions are a signal that there is something yet to learn from an event. A lot of negative emotion is held when we blame or project on to other people; this isn't to beat ourselves up but instead to acknowledge how we avoid confronting what we need to hear.

So, next time you find yourself in a difficult situation, or going over a painful memory, ask yourself, "What is it I need to learn from this event?" If you need to, scribble the learnings down on a pad by the side of your bed. After five or ten minutes turn the light back off and you'll be surprised to notice you are able to sleep with the emotion no longer plaguing you.

You can also practice this by intentionally conjuring a painful memory in order to learn from it and then release it.

Take a moment to think of a memory that has some stored negative emotion—frustration or annoyance is a good one to pick at first, nothing too serious.

Now flow back into the past. Go down into that memory, at first looking through your own eyes: notice what emotion you experience. Once you've experienced that, emotion label it out loud, then allow yourself to float up above the event so you are now looking down on it from above, so high that you're not even in the room or the car or under the canopy of the trees. Float so high that you're in the sky, even in the clouds, so high the emotion disappears completely.

Once you've noticed the difference between the strength of the emotions in the event looking through your eyes, and the neutral state of being detached looking down on the event, allow yourself to come back to now. Float down into your body, your room, and open your eyes.

This technique is what Time Line therapists use to allow client's to let go of negative emotions from the past and by using the question (when in a detached state), "What is it you need to learn from this event, the learning of which will allow you to let go of the negative emotions?"

This technique can also be used to help you let go of limiting beliefs that you have which inhibit your progress towards your goals and aspirations. For managing bigger negative emotions in the past, or trauma, make sure you visit an appropriate therapist, preferably one trained in "Timeline Therapy".

Now let's take a look at spiritual detachment and how leaning in this direction can help you develop greater emotional resilience both in the short and long term.

SPIRITUAL DETACHMENT

Detachment means letting go of attachment to things, people, places, experiences, and events; easy to say but more challenging to do.

Spiritual detachment comes from being able to realise our true essence or nature as being the awareness of our thoughts, feelings, or emotions rather than being those thoughts, feelings, emotions, or experiences themselves.

To give an example of this take a look at your hand for a moment then consider that physiologically every single cell in your hand wasn't there a year ago. In fact, every single cell in your body is replenished over an eighteen-month cycle and ninety-percent within twelve months...

This literally means you're becoming the new person with a brand new body every twelve to eighteen months or more accurately moment to moment!

So now, when you look in the mirror, consider how you know that it's you? If every single cell in your body has changed over the last eighteen months, how do you recognise you as you?

The answer that we are inevitably led to in time is the reason that we know it is us is because we are aware. Your essential nature is awareness, not your body or your mind, but your awareness of your body and mind and everything else your senses process.

Awareness is the essence of what makes us human. This is such a subtle yet vitally important discovery for human evolution.

In Eknath Easwaran's classic interpretation of the ancient spiritual text the *Bhagavad Ghita*, he describes the ghita, talking about the "field" and the "knower of the field". This is quite an amazingly modern description of reality considering what Quantum Physicists are now saying about the nature of the universe. According to them, there is no difference at the quantum level between matter and energy. In fact, the more reading you do around spirituality and quantum physics, the more you begin to realise that what ancient sages have been saying for thousands of years is now being realised scientifically. It really is an astonishing time to be alive right now.

Back in the early 1980s, an amazing physicist, David Bohn, was part of a TV panel of religious, spiritual, and scientific figures discussing the nature of reality. There is an amazing moment where David talks for approximately eighteen minutes uninterrupted (the audience and other panelists are so quiet you can hear a pin drop) about the nature of existence and life.

The most alarming (and reassuring at the same time) thing is that the Dalai Lama is sat next to him nodding and smiling all the way through.

When we begin to realise our true selves as the knower of the body and the mind, the knower of the field, as the Bhagavad Ghita puts it, then at that point we can begin to take the journey toward detachment from the ups and downs of life. We begin to become the witnesser of the events unfolding in front of us as opposed to being anchored into the experience itself and what it is doing to us. Pain, pleasure, like, dislike, all of these begin to have less sway as we learn more and more about who we really are.

All events are neutral, in reality. This may seem controversial or even insensitive. How can, for example, the physical abuse of a child be considered neutral? It is not possible, of course, at the human level to answer that question. No one in their right mind would ever argue against the abuse of children being a horrific immorality.

We can see how in the process of human evolution that it is trauma and difficult experiences that led to development. One of the most fulfilled women I ever met was at the side of a par three on a golf course (you know how much I love my golf). There was a delay in play as it was a busy golf day and this was the charity hole were you got to pay money to charity and if you hit the green or indeed made a hole in one you won a prize. I spent time talking to the lady who was the founder of the charity; she explained that she had lost her daughter to this rare cancer and this had created the foundation of the charity. What amazed me at the time was the lightness of her essence; she was an amazing human being who had transmuted her suffering for the greater good of mankind. There are so many amazing examples of this in life: think of the recent experience of Rob Burrows and his family and the wider Rugby League family in generating awareness around Motor Nerone Disease. I can recommend Deepak Chopra's book here, *The Seven Spiritual Laws of Success*, for help considering how your own life may have clues to your deeper purpose.

There are so many factors involved in the making or breaking of a person, but ultimately, it is we (or more accurately our minds) who interpret events as good or bad. Our higher self can simply be aware that we are processing an event which causes us to feel something and allow that to be pass without creating more turbulence or action. If we do feel compelled to act, we can do so with dharma. We can make it our purpose to create something positive for mankind from something previously deeply troubling. Simply judging events and feeling bad ourselves in time we begin to realise serves absolutely no purpose whatsoever other than to take you away from your own peace.

These are challenging concepts for many on the personal development path and learning to detach from the immediate ups and downs of life is a good starting point. The more we detach, the more we will see they are not really ups and downs, they are just events that are, for the most part, out of our control.

FACING DEATH

Death is one of the primary fears of mankind, yet spiritual and scientific knowledge can help us let go of even this supreme fear.

Knowing the nature of the body helps us come closer to the truth. For a start, we are simultaneously living and dying in every moment. Trillions of cells are dying and being brought to life inside our body every second of every day. We are therefore a walking example of life and death at the same time. We breathe in, we breathe out. Breathing in draws oxygen into our lungs, which keeps us alive. Breathing out breathes out carbon dioxide, which is harmful. And yet, it is the oxygen that slowly erodes and ages us, and the greater our tolerance for carbon dioxide, the fitter and healthier our bodies are… So, there is life in death and death in life. We are walking paradoxes of the first order.

The *Bhagavad Ghita* shines further light:

"Though it seems to live in the land of mortals and undergo change and death, the real knower in every creature is deathless, hidden in the heart..."

This "knower" can be described as the soul, spirit, or simply the awareness that we described earlier. The body's cells come and go as will your body, but the awareness—the soul, the spirit—of the body? I will let you draw your own conclusions what happens to that, albeit it is difficult to imagine the death of something so esoteric.

A classic phrase from A Course In Miracles comes to mind, "Nothing created can be destroyed". All that is is the formless unmanifest energy which simply *changes form*. If you burn a tree to the ground, the tree is still there, it has simply become ash.

Whatever you believe, we can all acknowledge what an amazing gift this life is. Even its most troubling and difficult experiences are usually in order to help us grow. We can do so with joy, with reverence, with peace. And, with greater detachment comes greater resilience to what previously may have set us back or even destroyed us emotionally.

ACTIONS & REFLECTIONS FROM CHAPTER 13

If you have not already, why not try reading a spiritual book? You could start with Deepak Chopra's *The Seven Spiritual Laws of Success* or Eckhart Tolle's *A New Earth* or Mickey Singer's *The Untethered Soul* or indeed the aforementioned book by Eknath Easwaranath (albeit I would suggest you try others first).

Whether you are deeply interested in spirituality or just getting started, this material may well help with the development of a practice of meditation which, whether you are religious or not, will massively assist you in your journey towards greater detachment, awareness, and Emotional Resilience...

CHAPTER FOURTEEN
Emotion and Physiological Pain

One of the most exciting developments in the personal development world for me has been the growing link between emotions stored in the body and physiological pain. I have witnessed both in groups and with my 1:1 clients what previously I would have described as a miracle.

Here is an example of a client experience I had before becoming proficient in working with the Pain Paradigm (our way or releasing chronic pain with Time-Line Therapy). I share this story as it illustrates how, through curiosity and a willingness to experiment, my client was able to get results and make headway.

Around 2015, a client came to see me with back pain. A few of his colleagues had been clients of mine from a business perspective, albeit the nature of coaching is that personal realisations often come along the way towards our professional goals! They had suggested to him that he gave it a go.

He explained that having seen all manners of physical therapists, he was still experiencing pain when cycling and, as an Ultra Man (an incredible endurance athlete), this was a problem for him. He also said he didn't have much hope for our work together, however, a number of his colleagues had suggested he come and see me. So, after an initial introduction, I explained I would be happy to go through the process which I follow and see what happens without any promises of an outcome.

What we found, during the process of a detailed clarity coaching process, was someone who didn't really experience emotion. He was living in an entirely detached manner psychologically.

On the MBTI personality preference test, people who tend to view life from a detached perspective are psychologically viewing themselves in the picture when thinking about events rather than living events through their own eyes.

People with this trait have more of a Thinker preference on the MBTI profile and those who experience greater emotion (living events through their own eyes) and using those feelings in decision making have a greater Feeler preference. No surprises here. It also won't surprise you that the vast majority of CEOs and MD's in business are also much higher Thinker preferences than Feeler. This is how they are able to make decisions which affect so many people's lives without empathetically being as affected by those decisions.

In my client's case, he did indeed have a very strong Thinker preference. He wasn't experiencing emotion or any feelings really (he told me he didn't cry) and after all, detaching from feelings and sensations is pretty useful for an ultra-endurance athlete.

My suspicion as a therapist at this stage was that some unresolved or unexperienced emotion was coming out in the body, having no other outlet.

So after a full detailed personal history and subsequent time line therapy intervention we found that a simple task helped my client overcome the pain which went immediately from an eight out of ten to a three out of ten. Interestingly, there are links between the task I assigned him and what I have subsequently learnt about the Pain Paradigm and how to reduce and in some cases eradicate chronic pain using this methodology.

I asked my client each and every time he experienced physiological pain on the bike to label the emotion in the body. What he found, to his amazement, was that he was actually experiencing *anxiety*, not pain, which he was previously unaware of. He learned that he wasn't ever really present on the bike: he was always thinking about the future, his time, the finish, and a host of other things. By learning to use pain as a signal to re-associate into his feelings, the pain became at first manageable, and in time, meaningless.

I share this because for those who don't tend to experience emotion, there could either be some subconscious repression occurring or subconscious detachment (as opposed to consciously choosing to detach), and if this is the case, then learning to feel and experience our emotions is key to being able to rise above them and let go as opposed to ignoring them.

I knew we had made progress when my client later shed tears as a result of empathetically feeling emotion linked to some of his new wife's past experiences. I wouldn't normally "celebrate" tears, and yet in this context it was a key step forwards in his personal development journey.

Associating into our emotions is also, paradoxically, a great tool to help us learn how to detach and release them! As Tad James, the creator of Time Line Therapy, says: "You cannot let go of something you are not aware of."

Before I make some recommendations for any of you experiencing chronic pain, let's share a couple of client interventions involving releasing chronic pain using the Pain Paradigm process.

∼

BEN IS a long term business coaching client and in one particular session he wasn't his usual self. Just before I went for a comfort break, I asked him what was the number one current cause of stress in his life. When I got back, he surprised me by saying that it was his wife's back pain, which had exacerbated recently, and meant she was in so much pain she couldn't get out of bed.

At the end of our session, I suggested that his wife book an online call with me, as there was a chance that at least a percentage of the back pain could be linked to repressed emotion, which I could potentially be able to help her with. I also explained that there was a simple test we could do to ascertain whether that was the case, so that we would know pretty quickly in the session if there was anything I could do to help.

A day or two later (she was understandably keen to speak to me as soon as possible), the time of the session arrived. I asked the questions which elicit whether pain is linked to emotion and checked in with her on the level of her pain which changed as a result of my questions. This was the signal that demonstrated that there was a link between the pain being experienced and repressed emotion stored in the body. What happened next blew my mind, in many ways, as it was one of my first experiences of actively working with the Pain Paradigm with a client, and certainly my first experience of doing so online.

Over the next half an hour, I helped Sarah become aware of the link between the pain and the emotion and as a long list of emotions came up the level of pain continued to diminish, so much so that within half an hour her back pain had gone from an 8/10—in other words, seriously debilitating—to a zero! The pain was fully released and Sarah was able to walk around, stretch, and move in a way which amazed her.

∼

LET me share some of the theory behind how and why this works. Firstly, emotions which are suppressed (not fully expressed and allowed to be experienced) can become repressed, and when this happens continuously the repression of said emotions can cause muscle tightness. Prolonged muscle tightness over an extended period of time restricts blood flow which itself is excruciatingly painful. Often, when working with pain, there is a physiological element as well. However, most physiological pain ought to have healed by around three months, so chronic pain beyond three months—especially with back pain—is a signal that there could be some repressed emotion causing restricted blood-flow and pain.

Since this experience online with Sarah, I had a second opportunity to use the Pain Paradigm with a client who likewise was suffering back and shoulder pain. We had completed our detailed personal history and I wanted to make sure we were both fully aware of all the emotions in play before we completed our Time Line Therapy Intervention to release said emotions. Up to this point, I was relatively inexperienced with the Pain Paradigm, therefore I booked out ninety minutes to work in person with the client. Again what transpired surprised me.

Rather than the pain releasing easily, as had happened with Sarah, the pain first began to get worse and went up to a 10/10 before beginning to come down. I knew that this could happen as per my training, however, the surprise was what I learnt about my client in the process; things came up in what turned out to be a three hour session rather than ninety minutes. Much of what came up had not appeared in her detailed personal history. On the journey from the pain reaching a 10/10 and then eventually down to a 0, so many more significant emotional events resurfaced with associated emotions. This was challenging in terms of patience and perseverance but also amazingly liberating and made our Time Line Therapy Session the following month so much more powerful, knowing we were releasing and healing everything from the past.

Since those two early experiences, I have trained many groups of NLP Practitioners and Time Line Therapy Master Practitioners in the Pain Paradigm, including witnessing one amazing day of training where eighty-percent of the delegates left the room on day two of the training *pain free*. I did not know going into that course that so many of the delegates were experiencing chronic pain and any slight doubts I may have had at this stage about the Pain Paradigm and the benefit of it disappeared completely. I was convinced and have continued to experience what many would believe are miracles. One of the delegates took a photo of his wife's hands which changed colour as the blood flow returned to her hands as the pain released.

EMOTIONAL RESILIENCE

What can you do now if you are experiencing chronic pain?

Here is my challenge to you for the next week or so, practice, when you experience a moments discomfort, labelling what the emotion is. This helps in so many ways. Firstly, you will become more aware of subconscious patterns of thought and emotion, and secondly, you will begin to ask a question: Who is the person becoming aware of the guilt or frustration you just experienced? The answer, of course, is your true self, your essential nature, and by focusing your awareness on what the actual emotion is and where in the body it is located—and what size and shape it is all the important details—you are accessing your higher self and growing your awareness of an unconscious pattern of emotion. This exercise in itself can bring relief as you identify more space around the emotions which in the past may have seemed all-consuming.

Secondly, when experiencing acute pain, pause and get a pen and paper out, sit still, and ask yourself: what emotion am I feeling right now? Make sure you say the emotion aloud (thoughts are not emotions) and after each emotion, label the level of pain you are experiencing out of ten. If you can and do notice the level of pain change, be excited, as there is something you can do about it! If you are patient, you maybe able to diminish the pain significantly and—with perseverance—become pain free.

Finally, if you are experiencing long term chronic pain (especially if you have explored other avenues unsuccessfully), then it makes sense to find a Time Line Therapy Master Practitioner who can help you explore this avenue, both to become pain free and also let go of all scar tissue associated with past events.

There is also one more case study I would like to share which may help in a different way, this one involving grief.

∽

I WAS WORKING with a client who experienced a significant bereavement in between sessions and, although it wasn't appropriate to continue with the therapeutic intervention we had planned, what we were able to do was to tune in to the body and the emotions she was experiencing. This allowed her in the session to both label the emotions of sadness, loss, and grief, notice the size shape and movement of the emotion within the body, and also become aware of where the emotions were *not* in the body. There were many tears in the session and the client became aware of a "space around the emotions". She said it wasn't that the sadness had gone—nor should we expect it to—but more that she was now aware of a space and lightness around the emotion where as before everything was heavy and enveloping.

This methodology can be really useful for helping the grieving process (remember the emotions are just emotions and nothing to be afraid of) and also for those who have a tendency to react angrily. The ability, in these difficult moments, to tune into our feelings and become the witness of the emotions rather than the emotion itself—and the thoughts *around* the emotion—is key to developing greater emotional resilience.

An exercise to help grow awareness of your body and emotions. This is especially useful for those whom are naturally detached from emotion…

Sit comfortably. Choose an area of the body to become aware of and close your eyes. Begin to notice what you feel in that area of the body: is there any tension or relaxation, can you feel the energy within that part of the body? Spend a moment breathing into that part of your body and notice what happens, if anything...

Now place your awareness on your hands or feet. Keep your eyes closed and again notice the feeling in that area of your body and breathe energy into that area of your body. What do you become aware of?

Now shift your attention to the crown of your head. Place all your attention and awareness on that spot as again you breathe into that area. Again see what you notice. There are no right and wrong answers here, just the experience itself...

Now aim to move your awareness slightly out of the body so your focus is now slightly above the crown of your head; notice again what the experience is like, how you feel, and any sensations that are different or similar to your normal feelings/experiences.

This exercise helps us grow our awareness of the body and the energy in and around the body and our ability to consciously direct that energy.

CHAPTER FIFTEEN

Restoring Mental, Emotional, and Physical Energy

To achieve a balanced state in our mental, emotional, and physical energy buckets, it is essential to find an equilibrium that works for us. This equilibrium involves equal measures of movement, play, work, and rest, which ultimately contribute to our overall health and well-being. After all, feeling good in ourselves will have a colossal impact on every element of our lives. The first and most primary relationship we have is with ourselves, and if we get that right, and we feel good, then the others can follow on from that example.

In truth, achieving a successful life is a rarity because it requires mastering the art of balance and not sacrificing one area for another. We can all think of individuals who have sacrificed their health for material wealth or those who have sacrificed relationships for independence. The aim of this chapter is to assist you in finding the balance between mental, physical, and emotional energy.

Let's begin by considering the differences in how each type of energy is renewed:

- Physical Energy is rejuvenated through good nutrition and regular exercise.
- Mental Energy is replenished through fulfilling work and engaging in hobbies that we love.
- Emotional Energy is renewed through practices such as sleep, meditation, and activities that allow us to be fully present in the moment, free from the distractions of thoughts.

In truth, sleep rejuvenates all three energy types, as it is our master biorhythm that keeps us regulated in all areas. Scientifically, it has been proven that poor sleep affects our hormones, subsequently impacting our eating habits (the hormone ghrelin gets released if we don't sleep well, creating a sense of hunger) and sense of satiety.

Having read the above, take a moment to reflect on which area of your life could benefit from greater balance. Consider your answer when responding to the coaching questions at the end of this chapter.

Now, let's explore the concept of balancing "Being, Doing, and Having".

To-dos refer to the list of actions we feel obligated to take, while *to-be* represents the state of being we desire to live in. Allowing non-doing, that is, creating space for rest without distractions, enables us to experience more being. Often, our never-ending to-do lists hinder us from being fully present in the moment and enjoying the gifts of life. Time spent with loved ones, in nature, or engaging in other fulfilling activities can be compromised by a mounting sense of responsibility and our self-identity tied to various roles.

We may find it challenging to embrace non-doing as discomfort, past memories, emotions, and failures often arise during such moments. Consequently, many individuals choose to live in a constant state of distraction, avoiding confronting these challenges to relaxation and rest. However, without having balance as a goal, these patterns can remain unresolved, leading to a growing sense of unease which, if unchecked, can lead to dis-ease. More and more information is coming to light now linking stress and its role in causing inflammation in the body which over time—without healing—can lead to a number of physiological conditions.

So, what must we do? How can we effectively overcome this lack of balance in modern life?

First and foremost, seeking help from others is a clear and surefire way to approach this challenge. This involves tapping into one of the gateways towards higher consciousness: the courage to be vulnerable. Rest assured, you are not alone in facing these challenges.

Having a support system, a community, a coach, a therapist, or anyone who possesses the patience, compassion, experience, and capacity to hold space for you, can make a significant difference. They can guide when guidance is needed, assert direction when necessary, and provide hope when appropriate, especially when the goal is itself a more balanced and truly successful, healthy life!

Be aware that resistance may arise within you as your ego fights to preserve its sense of self by finding reasons to avoid addressing this issue. However, with hopeful optimism and realism, I can assure you that embarking on this path requires courage, support, compassion, and commitment. The journey involves realigning what is mismatched, reigniting what has been extinguished, and reconnecting with what truly matters, beyond conditioned behaviours and attitudes toward life usually centred on an outdated view of success based upon comparisons with others as opposed to what is truly right for you.

On the other side of this transformation lies a freedom you may have never experienced before. It grants you a sense of peace that you deserve but have long been deprived of. A newfound presence of mind that has been forgotten for far too long.

In short, on the other side of this process, you will find your new life. A life where the bar is set much higher than simply going through the motions. It is a life animated and driven by a state of aliveness, growth, connection, and a profound ability to breathe in, exhale, relax, reflect, appreciate, and experience life more deeply.

ACTIONS & REFLECTIONS FROM CHAPTER 15

A. Begin by asking yourself: What are you best at—starting things, changing things, or stopping things? Once you have the answer, identify what you are worst at among the remaining two options. For instance, someone who excels at starting things may struggle with stopping or changing things.

Once you identify your weakest area, ask yourself the following questions and allow whatever arises to come forth:

- If starting: What is it that I am not being that I want to be?
- If changing: What is it that I am not doing that I want to do?

- If stopping: What is it that I am not having that I want to have?

B. Engage in a stop/start review:

- What is it that you need to start doing?
- What do you need to do more of?
- What do you need to do less of?
- What do you need to stop doing?

C. Utilise Cartesian coordinates (useful for decision making around creating balance):

- What happens if you do?
- What happens if you don't?
- What doesn't happen if you do?
- What doesn't happen if you don't?

Note: Allow time to contemplate the last two questions, as they often lead to transformative insights and "aha" moments.

Additionally, we suggest considering the following pursuits:

- Personal development in any form, such as reading a book, taking a course, attending therapy or coaching sessions.
- Cultivating habits like reading, meditation, spending time in nature, engaging in yoga/stretching/exercise, and pursuing specific hobbies. Choose one or two to focus on initially and intend to create a window of time for you each day even if it is just five minutes a day for you!

Reading is beneficial for personal growth, for pleasure, and for sharing knowledge that may be valuable to others. Meditation allows the mind to find the equivalent of a gym for the muscles, providing time for self-care and overcoming any guilt associated with prioritising oneself.

Spending time in nature, feeling the wind, observing the sights, and listening to the sounds, grounds us each day. Engaging in stretching or exercise, combined with nature for some, helps establish a sense of stability. For example, if stretching is something that you want to prioritise for you, enabling beliefs could include: "Stretching nourishes my body", "It makes me feel good", and "It allows me to move with vitality and carry out daily tasks comfortably".

Furthermore, consider pursuing hobbies that don't require digital devices, such as fishing, footy, swimming, tennis, dance, painting... Enabling beliefs in this case might include: "I love my time engaged in my chosen hobby", "Time passes quickly when I am involved", and "I feel refreshed after spending time on my hobby."

Remember, finding balance and transitioning from doing to being is a journey. Be patient with yourself, and utilise the suggested coaching actions along the way. It is through this process that you can unlock a new level of freedom and experience a truly fulfilling life.

CHAPTER SIXTEEN

Developing Emotional Resilience as an Attitude

When we appreciate that our attitude is formed from our core values, and that each value has a number of key beliefs associated with it which in turn create our attitude, we begin the journey of taking responsibility for our own Emotional Resilience through developing both greater awareness and knowledge of our own values and beliefs and how we can change beliefs and values which don't work for us to support greater emotional resilience and wellbeing.

Let's more closely examine the distinctions between values, beliefs, and attitudes.

VALUES

Values are guiding principles that dictate our behaviour and actions. They represent what we consider important and desirable. For example, some people might value honesty above all, while others might place a higher emphasis on ambition, loyalty, or compassion. We usually inherit our values from our family, culture, religion, or personal experiences, and they become the compass that directs our decisions and reactions.

When it comes to emotional resilience, understanding our values is vital. Values act as an anchor, providing stability during times of emotional turmoil. For example, if someone values peace and harmony, they may have a strong resilience towards conflicts or confrontations, aiming to resolve such situations calmly and amicably.

Moreover, aligning our actions with our values can foster emotional well-being. Discrepancies between values and behaviours can lead to internal conflicts and emotional distress. In contrast, living in accordance with our values can instil a sense of purpose, fulfilment, and emotional balance.

BELIEFS

Beliefs, on the other hand, are the convictions or acceptance that certain things are true or real. They are the assumptions we hold to be true about ourselves, others, and the world around us. Our beliefs significantly impact our interpretation of events, shaping our thoughts, feelings, and behaviours.

In terms of emotional resilience, our beliefs can either fortify or weaken it. For instance, if we hold the belief that we are capable of overcoming adversity, this can promote resilience by encouraging a proactive and positive approach to challenges. On the contrary, if we believe that we are victims of our circumstances, we may respond to hardships with despair and helplessness, hampering our emotional resilience.

Furthermore, beliefs about emotions themselves play a crucial role. If we perceive certain emotions as "bad" or "unacceptable", we may resist or suppress them, causing emotional imbalance. By believing that all emotions are valid and provide useful information, we can better navigate our emotional landscape, thus enhancing our resilience.

CHANGING VALUES AND BELIEFS

Recognising that some of our values and beliefs may be hindering our emotional resilience is the first step towards change. Neuro-Linguistic Programming (NLP) can help us identify, challenge, and modify unhelpful beliefs as well as to improve both our career (Motivational Maps are incredibly useful in this area), relationships, health or quite frankly any area of life that is causing an issue for you.

Changing deeply ingrained values and beliefs requires trust, authenticity, vulnerability, and courage, albeit by exploring in this way you can transform your attitudes, cultivate emotional resilience, and pave the way for a more satisfying and balanced life.

TYPICAL ISSUES WITH VALUES:

Lack of balance in life:

As a Trainer of NLP Coaches and therapists, we often see people coming to work who have a lack of balance in life. As much as they try to make a change to their habits and behaviours, they find that willpower only lasts for so long before they return back to the previous unwanted behaviour. My previous career in the Leisure and Fitness industry demonstrated this pattern to me year after year, with thousands of new gym members every January tailing off their good intentions before Spring had arrived.

In this context, working on eliciting life values will a) give you an insight into why you are out of balance as you begin to see how your unconscious priorities are out of alignment with your conscious intention and b) give you the opportunity working with an NLP coach to change your unconscious values to match your goal or c) dare I say it: quit the goal and set a goal which is more in alignment with your values as they are.

Conflict in Relationships

If you spend enough time focusing on relationships and they are one of your top five life values (we only ever seem to get time to focus on five core values in life), then it is worth exploring what values are present within your relationship values. The upcoming case study with Mark is a good example of how someone's values around relationships can cause an issue. Remember, your values stem from your experiences in life and Mark's scar tissue had caused the development of values and beliefs which essentially were trying to help him avoid the pain he had previously experienced in relationships. Overcoming this pattern was another step in Mark's healing journey to be able to create the loving relationships he wanted in his life.

Mark came to see me to help him to overcome his pattern of anger and emotional outbursts, which historically had plagued his relationships both personally and professionally. He had strained relationships with his family, business colleagues, and a string of now ended relationships with friends and ex-partners.

Throughout the first eight months of working together, Mark was able to understand where the anger was coming from (an unconscious desire to protect himself from being hurt again—better to reject than be rejected) and through the therapeutic process Mark was able to heal the past scar tissue. This wasn't, however, the big breakthrough Mark was looking for, as issues still persisted. The true breakthrough only came when together Mark and I explored his values and beliefs around relationships.

In that session, what we found was that Mark's top five values were all underpinned by the desire to protect him from being hurt...

His values included:

- Reliability (Not being let down)
- Loyalty (Also not being let down)
- Making the effort (*Not* not being there for me)
- People having my back (not being disingenuous)

Throughout the coaching journey Mark had begun to understand this truism that you get what you focus on in life, and if you focus on what you don't want, you get more of it. We all get this at some level yet almost all of us struggle to apply to our lives.

We wouldn't teach our kids to try not to fail their exams, or to try not to miss a penalty playing kids football, yet how many people on the planet are still struggling to try and lose weight or stop being poor!

How many people are trying to avoid conflict and, in doing so, create it.

Knowing this, we were able using some NLP techniques to change Mark's relationship values to be about the things which he wants to bring to relationships: kindness, acceptance, love, and joy. In doing so, he created a completely different attitude, which in turn reinforced a much more Emotionally Resilient way of life.

Knowing now what we do about attitude and its psychological components, it is time to begin to explore consciously and develop a value of Personal Development and Awareness (something that motivates you to continue the personal development journey) and a set of subsidiary values and beliefs which support you on that journey.

ADDITIONAL CONTEXTS FOR VALUES WORK:

Poor health Behaviours

For the person who spends enough time focusing and thinking about health (I'm thinking of the person who is constantly dieting yet not getting anywhere), do you know that less than 2% of people who aim to lose weight do so successfully and keep it off for five years?

If the above sounds familiar then exploring your heath values could well be the key for you. The failed dieter is consistently running a pattern of "away from" motivation driven by the desire to lose weight (rather than, for example, the desire to "get healthy")! The problem in life is that you consistently get what you focus on, and the unconscious mind doesn't process negatives very well, so in the same way that if you say to yourself "Don't fail" your mind hears "FAIL" loud and clear, having values around health that are about losing what you don't want keeps giving back to you, in the long run, what you do not want. So what to do? Working with an NLP coach can help you let go of the values which are focusing on what you don't want and replace them with values which have positive behaviours and beliefs associated with them.

As an example, changing your unconscious value of losing weight (which is what we call an "away from" motivation, as you're moving away from what you fear rather than towards what you want) to I want to exercise or eat well will deliver results as long as you also let go of any unwanted beliefs around healthy food or exercise. This way of working can help the you (and your coach) to develop goals and have values that motivate you towards supporting you in the realisation of those goals.

Challenges with finances

For those struggling with money, we often find there is a lack of focus on it. If it's not one of your top five or six life values, you simply won't focus on it, which isn't a problem if you have money but can be if you haven't. If this is the case, making it a priority/life value is the first step towards change, followed by working on your values and beliefs around money.

Or, if money *is* a priority for you, but that tends to come in the form of worry or anxiety, then diving straight into work around money values is the next natural step for you.

As a personal example, when I was in the process of setting up my coaching business, I went to see an NLP coach, as I was aware that my attitude to money could potentially be a sticking point in my success. I grew up in a loving family and was very fortunate in so many ways, however, there were arguments between my parents when they had their monthly finance meeting and I frequently overheard negative comments about people driving nice cars or living in big houses.

When my life values were elicited by the coach, we found that money was not even in my top sixty life values. In fact, I never even mentioned it, even when my coach was pointing out that my goal was to run a successful BUSINESS! He kept stressing the point until eventually he just had to come out a say it: if I was going to run a successful business, I would need to focus on money. Obvious? In hindsight, yes, but these things frequently are obvious once we are made aware of them, but until that time, we are stumbling around in the dark.

As a result of the conversation we moved money up into my top five life values. Hey presto, you may think, the issue was sorted. Not in my case, as I then felt terrible for two weeks between the sessions as I became aware of the negative beliefs I had around money surfacing. Focusing on money made me aware of my negative programming, which then led to me working with my NLP coach again to let go of the limiting beliefs I had around money which I was now consciously aware of.

The outcome was that I was then able to enter into the start of my coaching and (soon-to-become) training business with a sense of peace and alignment around making money through helping other people as opposed to being conflicted around it. I have over the years met so many coaches, trainers, and therapists who are passionate about helping people yet who cant (as I couldn't initially) get comfortable either charging for or valuing their time sufficiently as a coach to make a viable business out of it. Did you know for example that only 10% of trained coaches ever actually get paid for coaching! The problem here is coaches paying too much attention focusing on others and not enough time exploring their own values, beliefs and attitudes to make sure they start with alignment or at least find alignment along the way.

ACTIONS & REFLECTIONS FROM CHAPTER 16

Begin an emotional resilience journal.

1: Journal what emotions came up today: name it, identify where was it in the body and what was the trigger. If you can go a stage further, see if you can identify where this emotion first came from. Was the trigger actually opening up a wound from the past or was it that someone crossed a core value of yours?

2: Decide to become aware of values and beliefs which maybe challenging your journey to emotional resilience. Which area of life do you become most triggered in? Is it around money, relationships, work, health, or balance in life?

3: Once you have identified the core area for initial focus, ask yourself what is important to you about the one you have chosen and list your current values (aim to get as many as possible)…

- Once you have as many values written down as possible, circle your top eight most important values

- Now quickly order the values from 1 - 8 in order of most to least importance
- Now test your list against each other. For example, if you could only have x or y when waking up tomorrow which would you choose?
- At the end of this process, having tested each against each other, you will have a fairly accurate list of what your top values are in the area of life (or life itself) which you have chosen to explore

4: Now you have your list of top values—which have been tested—take a closer look at your top five. We only tend to have enough capacity in life for five priorities in each area of life important to us and indeed only sufficient capacity for five life areas we can focus upon at any time.

Take a look at each value in turn and consider the following questions?

How do I feel when I contemplate this value? Do I feel light or heavy, uplifted or under pressure, inspired or under a sense of obligation?

Does it feel like this value is helping you move towards the life you want or do you feel like this value was created unconsciously to help you to avoid judgement or failure?

What is important to you about this value? Notice the words that come up and again whether they are *facing* reality or about *avoidance* or something *not* happening.

What do you believe about this value? Journal the beliefs and take a look at what you notice: is this value supporting you to move towards your dreams and goals or not?

Finally begin to think about what values would support you on your journey towards your goals. Consider getting in contact with an NLP coach to help you realign your values to create the alignment and as a result resilience which you desire.

CHAPTER SEVENTEEN
Love

In the initial scoping out of this book, this chapter was absent. However, as we went through the editing process, we started to receive some feedback from our coaching community, and it became apparent that it would be a useful final chapter for this book. Indeed, when I shared the front cover and the title with our community, I received lots and lots of feedback and commentary. What I hadn't shared with people was that the front cover of the book was actually a painting by my mother and which has deep personal meaning for me. Not all of the comments were entirely positive, although there was lots of useful advice about the title.

We have all sorts of coaches and specialists in our network, some of whom have specialisms in business development and marketing (not areas of strength for me!). Rather than taking any offence at the feedback, I felt an overwhelming sense of love. I couldn't believe the amount of people who took the time out of their day to offer advice, guidance, and support in an attempt to help me make the maximum impact with this book. I experienced an overwhelming sense of care and support from these amazing people.

Around the time this feedback was coming in, I was also listening to one of my favourite authors, Wayne Dwyer, on my way into court for two weeks of jury duty. It was the combination of these elements which led to the formation and development of this chapter.

LOVE AS AN EMOTION:

There is a theory within the personal development world that there is only one true emotion and that that emotion is Love. At first glance, this idea seems preposterous, as we all can think back to times when we have experienced if not all then the majority of the negative emotions discussed in this book and perhaps some that are not. So, how then can it be true that there is only one true emotion?

Perhaps the key to this philosophy is the word "true". It isn't to deny the existence of the other emotions but instead to question the truth of them. At the heart of this idea is the link between Love and spirituality or for those more religious the link between Love and God. If everything was created by God and everything is God—and Love is God—then that also means that everything is Love. If this is true —I urge the cynics to suspend their disbelief for just a moment—then what of those other emotions? After all, anger or rage certainly do not feel like love, so where do they come from?

All things are either moving *towards* Love or *away* from Love. The uncomfortable emotions we experience are therefore a result of moving away from Love.

Take a look at the descriptions below and see what you make of the descriptions.

- Anger is felt when you perceive the injustice of lack of Love directed in your direction
- Sadness is associated with the perception of loss of Love either through death or loss of relationship.
- Fear represents the potential for loss of Love in many forms, either romantic relationships, or through the recognition we get from work or a certain role we play.
- Hurt comes from the removal of Love from someone we previously felt it from, either momentarily through a harsh comment or more permanently through a separation.
- Guilt and Regret are felt as a result of our own response to situations and stimuli where we are not proud about our own non-loving response.

So, if this philosophy is true, the nice thing is that there is a really simple solution to each and every personal development issue: LOVE!

LOVE YOUR ENEMY

As I was listening to that Wayne Dwyer book on the way to jury duty, he began to tell one of his favourite stories, one he gets quite emotional talking about. This is a story about St Francis of Assisi.

St Francis was terrified of lepers and at that time there were plenty of lepers roaming the streets with a bell attached to them so people could hear them coming and avoid contact socially (because seeing them was unpleasant) and physically (so that they could avoid the chances of contracting what was an incredibly contagious disease).

As the story goes, St. Francis was terrified of lepers and one evening, when in his evening contemplations/meditations, he was visited by Christ who told him when he was on his way to town tomorrow he would meet a leper on the road and that he was to both embrace and kiss this leper full on the lips! The following morning came and he was walking into town with St. Benedict who, on hearing the tale, said they should walk the other way into town! An eminently pragmatic response to a divine vision!

I am sure we can all relate with St. Benedict to a lesser or greater extent. However, such was St. Francis's devotion that he insisted on only walking the same way. He did indeed meet a leper—a child, in fact—and both embraced and kissed said Leper. He then proceeded to carry the leper into town. On reaching town, he went to retrieve the child from under his heavy shawl only to find that the child had disappeared! He never experienced leprosy and his fear of the disease disappeared in that very moment.

Whether you believe the story or not, it serves to illustrate that St. Francis was willing—despite his phobia—to move *towards* Love rather than away from it. St. Francis's faith in Christ was such that he was prepared to kiss the leper even knowing he might contract the disease.

So, how can we move in this direction in our own lives to experience more love and less of the uncomfortable emotions we have discussed? Well, the great spiritual and personal development teachers across the globe all agree on loving your enemy. This is what St. Francis did. He embraced and kissed his so-called enemy.

EMOTIONAL RESILIENCE

As I write this book, two of my coaching clients are going through tricky situations with their partners. One is going through a separation and the other is doing his best to navigate appropriate childcare arrangements for access to his daughter following a separation some years earlier.

In these situations, it is so easy to make the other person into the enemy. But the reality is, the only way to move forward is to Love them. To avoid confusion, we are not talking about romantic Love, here. We are talking about something far richer, deeper, and more universal.

Take a moment now to reflect and consider if there is anyone in your life whom you have conflict with — it could be a partner, a child, someone at work, or a person in your social life or sports life.

Write down a list of those people in your life who challenge and trigger you emotionally.

Now that you have your list, we can move on to the next step. One of my favourite actions from the Joseph DaSilva's book and personal development course, The Silva Method, is one whereby you induce a deeply relaxed state in yourself using self-hypnosis or what could be described as meditation techniques. Once in this "alpha state", you imagine the person or the people whom you are in conflict with and send them Love, surrounding them in white light. Once you have done this you move on to imagining conversations or situations working out amicably and crucially your attitude being one of calm, peace, and Love.

Visualisation, as we have discussed in previous chapters, is extraordinarily powerful. Your brain cannot tell the difference between these visualisations and reality, especially when you are in a deeply relaxed semi-dream state. By performing these visualisations, you are reprogramming your brain to see the world through eyes of Love and to look for positive solutions rather than thriving on conflict.

I wholeheartedly believe in this technique for diffusing conflict and navigating your way through life with peace, empathy, and Love. Try it and notice the positive differences in your life both in terms of you feeling lighter and your ability to navigate circumstances more effectively. Don't be surprised if you witness a miracle as well. Remember, the world is just energy reacting to the energy you put out!

Let me provide a couple of examples from my own life where I have experienced both sides of this coin.

Firstly, let me describe an event of which I am not particularly proud (I have, of course, forgiven myself since). I—and everyone in my business—are proud members of the Motivational Map Community of coaches, trainers, and consultants, and at various times we communicate and collaborate about the product, the Motivational Map itself. During one such occurrence, I was communicating on e-mail. As Maya Angelou once said, "You won't remember what they said or did, but you will remember how it made you feel." I can't remember the specifics of the situation or what we were discussing other than I disagreed with the direction or the response I had received. As a result of this, I felt a sense of frustration and annoyance and I penned a response to the e-mail I had received whilst feeling that sense of frustration. As an NLP trainer and Master Practitioner, we are trained in both hypnotic language patterns but also the ability to use laser like specific language. So, using my skills, I penned a response making my points well (eloquently, I thought) and being really careful not to write anything which could cause any offence by the recipient. I did so in a little bit of a rush and with a sense of urgency. I read the e-mail to check it over once and then sent it.

The following day I received a response to my e-mail which blew me away. I had indeed offended the recipient and in the process it seamed damaged a relationship with someone whom I admire and value in our life and business for many reasons. I took a step back re-read my e-mail and found that I hadn't said anything in the e-mail which you could take offence at (not in my model of the world, anyway). This caused even further frustration as my ego took hold and told me so many reasons why there was no reason to react like that and how I hadn't done anything wrong! Internally, though, something inside of me told me there was a key personal development moment in this experience for me. It didn't take long to arrive. In a conversation that day with a fellow coach they reminded me it is not the action or the words themselves that causes the response or the reaction it is *the energy behind those actions*. I knew this immediately to be true as this was the only hint of conflict in my professional life for a number of years and what was different was simply that I had communicated from a place of frustration as opposed to my normal resting relaxed peaceful state.

∼

Here is a second example, from the other end of the spectrum.

A few years back, we were at the time focusing on business growth and had partnered with a good friend of mine to help us both strategically and to make the most of our sales and marketing opportunities. After working together for a period of months, it appeared from our perspective that the partnership wasn't working as well as we would have liked and we took the tough decision to part ways (from a business partnership perspective, not as friends).

After the end of the partnership, we received some "not very nice" messages. It was in these moments that I realised that I have had a blessed, charmed life, as I had up to this point never experienced any form of verbal or physical abuse. The negative reaction from my friend was so severe that the severity itself made me pause and consider what must have been going on his end to react in this way. It certainly wasn't in keeping with how my friend normally reacts or behaves. So, as much as my ego wanted to judge, blame, and chastise, I did my best to remain neutral and not react to the accusations being thrown my way. This was one of the most uncomfortable periods of my life and I remember a key moment of advice that I received from a business owner in my network at this time. When I confided in him, he said, "Well, it's simple really: do you love him enough to put up with the shit?"

I knew the answer to that immediately: we had a long, positive history going back to childhood and had shared many positive life experiences along the way. I did not want to throw the friendship away.

There were plenty of learnings and nowadays our relationship is stronger than it has ever been,

ROMANTIC LOVE

Romantic Love for many conjures up images of film romance and phrases such as "You complete me". That vision of romantic Love is sadly setting people up for failure. What we all know really deep down is that Love comes from within!

Psychologically, we can actually demonstrate this, as it is possible using the NLP strategy of elicitation to elicit the sequence of internal representations (thoughts made up of visual, auditory, and kinaesthetic elements) that create the feeling of Love inside of us. What is alarming about this is that we begin to appreciate that what many of us consider as true Love is actually an internal sequence of thought which creates a feeling of Love internally in response to our Love sequence trigger being triggered by our partner!

If our relationships are built on this type of Love, then we are going to be set up for short term romances which burn bright and hot but which decline quickly as modern demands, other commitments, and life in general get in the way of our partner's ability to hit our buttons for us. I am a firm believer that this is the issue causing over two-thirds of marriages to fail, as most people in some way, shape, or form are looking for their partner to solve their own problems for them. In other words, without it necessarily being spoken, there is an unconscious expectation that the partner is responsible for making you feel good or make everything alright. This, of course, is too big a burden for anyone to carry and under that strain or weight the relationship begins to struggle as one or both partners find themselves walking on egg-shells trying desperately to avoid the negative triggers and trying to hit the right ones—if they have the energy and desire still to do so!

So what is the alternative? Well, in personal development, we have a phrase that you "either grow together or apart". This growth doesn't need to be linear, quick, or at the same pace, but personal growth is one of the hallmarks of successful relationships.

Contrast the situation above to a relationship where both parties knows to their bones that they are one hundred - percent responsible for their own emotional state and reactions to situations! All of a sudden, partners stop blaming their partner for the way they are processing the world and instead take responsibility for feeling good and also are able to apologise when they have a wobble (they are, after all, only human). Rather than co-dependancy, we now have co-independence, and what that creates is the space which allows relationships to be what they are meant to be.

Consider for a minute why it is that people go to music festivals, or go to watch live sport. Logically, you get a far better and more comfortable view watching the footy, cricket, or Glastonbury festival from the comfort of your living room, and yet people pay a lot of money and spend a lot of time travelling to enjoy such experiences. Why? Well, the reason is quite obvious: the experience. And what makes the experience? The atmosphere! Which is created by the people attending. It is the people at the events whose attendance magnifies the atmosphere to create a memorable event. This is where we start to see one of the purposes of relationships: "magnification". Relationships magnify what is there, they magnify the positive and likewise the less desirable elements of our character. So, when things are going smoothly and are at their most desirable, we will experience far greater pleasure with another than on our own. No euphemism intended here!

So, if the purpose of relationships is to magnify the more positive elements of life's experiences, what about the darker side of human existence? Relationships magnify our darker side and we see in others elements of our own shadow-side. As I am writing this, I am reminded of one of my favourite Deepak Chopra stories where he was setting up his holistic practice and moving away from more conventional medicine, which he had been practicing in the US. One of his first forays into this world was delivering workshops for fellow doctors, his peers if you like, and on one of these said workshops he was doing his best to make the point that anything we see outside of us has to be within, has to be part of our own psychological filters. In doing so, he was asking each of the doctors to carry out an exercise called the "mirror of relationships". In this exercise, Chopra asked each of them to think about someone they really liked and to write down all of the positive and negative character traits that this person exhibited. He then instructed them to do the same for someone whom they struggled to communicate with or whom they had conflict with…

After these initial instructions were carried out, Chopra continued to give instruction as to the mechanics of the mind and how we are all looking through our own filters at those whom we come across. At this point, one of his quite senior colleagues piped up saying, "Okay I kinda get this. I can accept that, you know, at times I can be a bit manipulative, a bit harsh, abrasive even, but what I can also say that I am absolutely not an 'idiot'."This was one of the words he had written down as a negative trait. The event was discussed and the workshop moved on.

About a week or so later, Chopra was giving the same doctor a lift home from the hospital. It was cold and snowy and so the doctor invited Chopra in for a cuppa. They both left the car and headed to the front door and the doctor was struggling to find his keys. He ended up rummaging in his bag looking for said keys and as he got more and more frustrated exclaimed, "What kind of IDIOT loses their keys on a day like this!?"

Moments later, he found said keys in the bottom of his bag and looked up to see Chopra beaming back at him. "What are you looking so smug about?"

"Nothing," Chopra replied.

In this example, we can see that anything we judge outside of us is actually a judgement of self. We judge others because deep down we would hate to be labelled in that way ourselves and how that would make us feel. This in turn can create fear as we avoid the perceived judgement of others.

So how does this relate to Love? Well, if the mirror of relationships is real—and from what I know about the mind's filters and how we can only see outside of ourself based on our own filters, it must be—then of course any Love we see outside of ourselves is also within us. In that sense, all Love of others is also Love of self!

When we start to understand at a deeper level who we really are, it starts to make more and more sense to let go of judgements and have the intention of loving unconditionally

ALL LOVE IS UNCONDITIONAL

When we think about Love there are often criteria or actions which need to be fulfilled in order to be rewarded with praise or affection. In Don Miguel Ruiz's book, *The Four Agreements*, he explains how we learn our own model of the world through the process of domestication. How our parents give and withdraw Love and affection on the basis of our ability as a child to conform to the rules of the family household and society. This is further anchored in through school years and indeed further ingrained in early business experiences. What this does is create the formation of the false self, the ego, that part of us that wants to fit in, that wants to experience pleasure of reward and avoid either the withdrawal of affection or direct punishment itself. This societal conditioning is deeply unconscious and our ego self then has a series of values and beliefs which seem real but, as we have discussed, are illusory. In truth, we are capable of anything, with unlimited choice in each and every moment. It is, however, this false unconscious self which creates the illusion of lack of choice. The coaches reading this book will be nodding along at this point as they carry out their role in helping their clients overcome their false self to become more in tune with their true self.

You may be thinking what has this got to do with Love? Well, *real* Love doesn't have any rules, it just is! There are no mandates that need fulfilling, no actions that need to be taken, no transactions to be completed. As far as real Love is concerned, it is an energy. It is the human mind that puts conditions in place and makes Love a transactional thing to be given and taken away; real Love cant be give or taken away, it just is.

"When the illusion of the false self falls away what remains is love."

Some of you maybe thinking well this is all well and good, Bevis, but what about boundaries and psychological safety. You are right. At one level of consciousness, having firm boundaries in place and being clear about those boundaries makes a lot of sense. Parents indeed need to create a safe space with boundaries for their children, albeit this can still be done with the energy of Love. Coaches can still encourage their clients to create safe boundaries in their relationships with the energy of Love and in business sometimes we need to hold firm and be true to ourself. This can be described as:

"Speaking words of truth with love."

In situations of conflict, there is a time to stick up for oneself. However, there is a big difference between avoiding conflict scenarios because we fear them or becoming triggered and angry and taking action from this place and speaking your truth with an energy of Love and peace and a detachment from the outcome. Remember, it is not the outcome that is important in these situations ,it is the conversation itself which is important. It is such a gift to give to others, for them to know that they can be themselves — including being upset or angry— and that you will be okay with that and won't judge them for it!

So, if all Love is unconditional, how you can take action now to benefit from the experience of greater levels of unconditional Love in your life?

The answer may surprise you, because it has nothing to do with the way that you act and has everything to do with the energy you are carrying moment to moment. In other words, how you feel. It is in this moment that we come full circle and finish where we started. To benefit from unconditional Love, we must learn to let go of, move through, and past old emotional scars, previous scar tissue, and judgement of self and others. We do this in order to be able to live a life of peace and Love whereby we don't have to *try* and act in a loving way, we simply see through a lens of

Love. Each time you become aware of a judgement of others or yourself, let it pass and use whatever personal development experiences you have access to—whether it be coaching, training, reading personal development books such as this, meditation, or time in nature—to allow you more and more regularly to enter into a state of peace, a state of Unconditional Love, where everything in that moment is as it should be. It always is, of course, it is just our egoic mind that will invent a reason otherwise!

Final Statement

As a final word, please remember the fundamental principle of this book: stress is not a thing, it is the body's physiological response to a trigger. In our modern lives, the trigger sets off a chain of thoughts or perceptions and feelings about events. The good news is we have more influence over our own thoughts and feelings than perhaps we thought previously!

In time, with practice, dedication, and support, you can grow your awareness, master your thoughts (which also means not taking them too seriously), and grow consciousness to a point where we can allow life to unfold, be unfazed by old triggers, and become light-hearted, generous, and kind to ourselves and others (rather than acting from guilt).

This book has taken some writing: it has been over five years in the making, largely down to a healthy dose of procrastination (not always a bad thing) and the realisation that releasing this book would be putting myself out there as me. I'm not hiding behind the label of being a coach or trainer or others in my team, this is me and my thoughts and beliefs as they stand presently, it is what I think and what consumes me day in, day out to help people on their own personal development journey to become emotionally resilient..

Some massive thanks are due to my good friend, Callum, without whom this project would never have been started, and to Tim, without whom it would never have been finished! To Joseph who has done an incredibly patient job bringing it to life in a readable format and to all of my clients friends and colleagues who have supported this in coming to life through our shared practice and experiences together From the bottom of my heart, thank you...

Work With Us

TO RECEIVE FURTHER SUPPORT, INFORMATION, AND HELP ON YOUR EMOTIONAL RESILIENCE JOURNEY PLEASE VISIT WWW.MAGENTACS.CO.UK

OR CONTACT US DIRECTLY AT: TEAM@MAGENTACS.CO.UK OR 0800 0096558

About the Author

Bevis Moynan is the only coach globally to be a Trainer of Neuro Linguistic Programming, a Senior Trainer of Motivational Mapping, and a Master Trainer of Time Line Therapy. This unique training, combined with decades of experience helping people 1:1 in groups and training other coaches and therapists in the Emotional Resilience Space, gave rise to this his second book, following *Mapping Motivation for Coaching*.